HIGH
JUNGLES
AND
LOW

HIGH
JUNGLES
AND
LOW

by

Archie Carr

Illustrations by Stephen Harris Carr
Foreword by Marjorie Harris Carr

UNIVERSITY PRESS OF FLORIDA

Gainesville/Tallahassee/Tampa/Boca Raton/
Pensacola/Orlando/Miami/Jacksonville

Library of Congress Cataloging-in-Publication Data

Carr, Archie Fairly, 1909–
    High jungles and low / by Archie Carr; with illustrations by
Stephen Harris Carr.
        p.   cm.
    Originally published: Gainesville: University Press of Florida,
1953.
    Includes index.
    ISBN 0-8130-1135-3
    1. Natural history—Central America.   2. Central America—
Description and travel.   3. Carr, Archie Fairly, 1909–
4. Naturalists—United States—Biography.   I. Title.
QH108.A1C37   1992   92–8969
508.728—dc20   CIP

The University Press of Florida is the scholarly publishing agency for the State
University System of Florida, comprised of Florida A & M University, Florida
Atlantic University, Florida International University, Florida State University,
University of Central Florida, University of Florida, University of North Florida,
University of South Florida, and University of West Florida.

University Press of Florida
15 Northwest 15th Street
Gainesville, FL 32611

Para vos, Margie

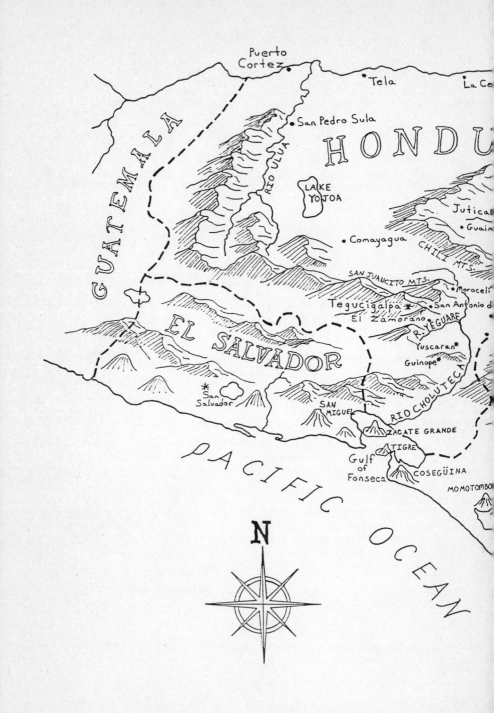

About the Author

RENOWNED sea turtle expert Archie F. Carr, Jr., was born in Mobile, Alabama, in 1909 and grew up in Fort Worth, Texas, and Savannah, Georgia. He received a B.S. from the University of Florida in 1932 and a Ph.D. in 1937 and taught at the University of Florida until his retirement in 1987, becoming the university's first Graduate Research Professor in 1959.

Between 1945 and 1949, he traveled all over tropical America, the West Indies, Australia, and Africa to study the ecology and migration of marine turtles. He spent 1956–58 on a leave of absence in Costa Rica as Catedrático de Biología, establishing a new Department of Biology in the country's expanded university. At that time he established a green turtle research camp at Tortuguero on the Caribbean coast of Costa Rica, which is continuing his research under the auspices of the Caribbean Conservation Corporation. He served as the corporation's technical director from its founding in 1959 and directed research at the research station. His book *The Windward Road* (1955) brought the world's attention to the endangered sea turtles in the Caribbean.

Operation Green Turtle, launched in the 1960s under Archie Carr's direction, distributed turtle eggs and hatchlings to nesting beaches in the Caribbean and the Gulf of Mexico. This work continues at the Carr Center for Sea Turtle Research set up at the University of Florida in 1986, the only research center in the world dedicated exclusively to the study of sea turtles.

His numerous awards and honors include the Daniel Giraud Elliott Medal from the National Academy of Sciences (1952) for his handbook on turtles; the O. Henry Memorial Award for a chapter from *The Windward Road* (1956); the John Burroughs Medal from the American Museum of Natural History (1957) for excellence in writing on natural history (specifically for *The Windward Road*); the World Wildlife Fund Gold Medal (1973); the Edward W. Browning Award from the Smithsonian Institution (1975); in 1978 he and his wife, Marjorie Harris Carr, each received the New York Zoological Society's Gold Medal for biological conservation; the Order of the Golden Ark from The Netherlands for biological research and conservation (1978); and the Hal Borland Award from the National Audubon Society (1984). Just before his death in 1987, he received the award of Eminent Ecologist from the Ecological Society of America.

Dr. Carr died at his home in Micanopy, Florida in 1987. He is survived by his wife, Marjorie, a conservationist, a daughter, Mimi, an actress, and four sons, Archie III, Stephen, Thomas, and David, all of whom are involved in natural history and conservation pursuits.

Contents

Foreword

IN *High Jungles and Low*, Archie Carr describes his abiding rapture with Central American landscapes, wildlife, and the people who live there. In the 1930s three exploratory trips into the Mexican wilderness had been so satisfying, so exhilarating and provocative, that we were more than ready for the move to Honduras in 1945. From the day we arrived with Chuck, a one-month-old babe-in-arms, and two-year-old Mimi (both slightly green from the sharp jolt of the airplane's rapid descent into the Valley of Tegucigalpa), until we reluctantly drove away four years later to Port of Cortez on the Caribbean coast of Honduras, with the addition to our family of two more sons, Stephen and Thomas, we knew we were in a special part of this earth and that we were fortunate beyond measure to be there.

To have a comfortable home, good domestic help with the cooking and the babies, spring-like climate, no biting insects that I can remember, and two horses saddled and waiting for us under the coyol palms at the back door every afternoon — what could be closer to heaven? And we said so to each other nearly every day.

Best of all we had time to become truly familiar with the broad, mountain-rimmed Yeguare River Valley on the Central America plateau. Again and again we followed the rocky quebradas up into the hills. We had a choice of a dozen different trails through the arid valley and up into the lovely pine forests of which Hondurans sing in their national anthem. Periodically, we climbed higher to the cloud forests on the mountain peaks and quietly absorbed the mysterious beauty of this unique landscape.

Whenever we visited the tiny abandoned silver mining town of San Antonio de Oriente or a small isolated farm, we would be soberly but cordially invited to dismount, have coffee, and visit awhile.

Dr. Karl Schmidt, a famous herpetologist, once wrote that naturalists make the best ambassadors because folks are pleased with your interest in their land, and therefore their natural suspicions toward a stranger are allayed. Perhaps this is why we always felt en rapport with country people — whether in Mexico, Honduras, Coata Rica, or any of the other small nations of the Central American isthmus.

The fascination and affection bred into Archie during our years in Honduras were nurtured and intensified during the next forty years by his yearly visits to Central America, particularly to Costa Rica, where he established the Green Turtle Research Station at Tortuguero on the Caribbean coast.

Archie was especially pleased with the advanced thinking on the part of the Costa Rican government in setting up a national park on the twenty-mile stretch of green turtle nesting beach at Tortuguero. He grieved, lost sleep, and was sorely perplexed about what to advise, what to say to local people who wanted to develop the coastline because they thought it would bring them an increased and steady income, something they desperately needed. How could he say, "Don't exploit your own resources for the fast buck"? How could he say, "Do as we say, don't do as we have done"? Conservation takes a lot of education anywhere. It requires people to take the long view. In Latin America it takes a special kind of message, and it is needed in massive doses, immediately.

By the greatest of good fortune, just as pressure reached a critical point to clear off the remaining woods for agricultural pursuits, build up the beach areas for tourist entertainment, and hunt out the dwindling supply of wildlife for sport or pretty coats, there has come into being a plan, *Paseo Pantera*, that is grand, audacious, and, moreover, feasible. It will ensure the long-range economic well-being of the local people while giving great pleasure to enormous numbers of ecotourists. And the complex associations of plants and animals that Archie found so beguiling will be set aside forever in a continuous greenbelt from Mexico to Panama.

All of Archie's sons have grown up to pursue careers in natural history and conservation, and his daughter, Mimi, an actress, has been an eloquent voice for conservation. There is a particular rightness in the fact that two of the young men promoting the regional conservation greenbelt plan are Archie's sons, Archie III (Chuck) and David. Chuck is coordinator for projects in Mesoamerica and the Caribbean Basin for Wildlife Conservation International, and David is executive director of the Caribbean Conservation Corporation, which continues to carry out the green turtle research and conservation in Costa Rica that Archie started thirty years ago. The organization has now enlarged its goals to include a whole new area of environmental education, conservation and land acquisition. In Chuck's words:

Paseo Pantera is a project to advance wild land conservation in Central America. It draws its substance from the land itself, from the unique origins and history of the Central American isthmus, a perspective that has been recognized but not implemented before in the region. During relatively recent geological time, tectonic upheavals in the crust of the earth forced up a bridge between the two immense continents of the Western Hemisphere. This was followed by one of the most dramatic events in the annals of biology. Paleontologists call the incident "The Great American Biotic Interchange." Plants and animals pushed their way in both directions across the landbridge, forever altering the composition of flora and fauna on both continents. Among the creatures traversing the new corridor, from north to south, were the Felids — the cat family — and the progenitor of the modern panther or cougar or puma, *Felis concolor*, a species that today is found in every continental country in the Western Hemisphere. Hence, *Paseo Pantera*: Path of the Panther.

In Central America, the biotic interchange left a distinctive legacy. North and South American plants and animals were smeared, if you will, in gradients, north and south along the length of the landbridge. Today, as a result, the kinds of plants and animals that you are likely to encounter at any given spot in Central America are mostly determined by how far you are from Texas or Colombia.

This phenomenon is *the* most interesting aspect of biology in Central America. It is what makes Central America unique in the world. It gives new justification for the world attention to conservation in the isthmus. From the story of the Great American Biotic Interchange, we may be able to draft a new, powerful agenda for conservation, one that would bind conservation action and advocates in every country from Panama to Mexico in common and hopeful purpose, an agenda to restore the landbridge.

Conservation of biological diversity is a fundamental component of the environmental movement. Setting up parks and other types of protected areas is a very direct, effective way to protect biodiversity. In Central America, parks are often too small to be secure safe-havens for species, yet, in many cases in the region, small parks can be made larger by joining them together at international frontiers. Isolated parks can be joined to other "islands" of habitat by implementing the idea of wildlife corridors. Where corridors do not exist because of human abuses, they can be restored. In the majority of cases, the land that will need restoration will be what is called "marginal lands," forbidding terrain where colonists should never have entered in the first place and whose repair will address fundamental economic development requirements, such as soil and water conservation.

Linking of parks and protected areas with wildlife corridors is inherently good thinking based on a very contemporary theory in the modern science of conservation biology. But in Central America, the concept is given particular credibility because the entire isthmus once served as the most imposing corridor in the history of the world. Together, the countries of Central America have the unique opportunity to unite in the purpose of restoring and preserving the landbridge as a biological wonder. They can do this in the name of the people of the world and will be justified in the expectation that the people of the world will rally to the ambitious cause.

A chain of parks in Central America, linked by corridors, would also establish a land-management matrix. This protected-area system, the *Paseo Pantera*, would begin to organize the landscape, helping to sort out where development could proceed responsibly, and where it would be inevitably doomed: the mountain ridges, the flood-prone riverbanks, the mangrove shorelines, the wetlands, the semi-deserts. These are the "marginal lands," a name coined by agriculture. *Marginal* to human use, perhaps, but *central* to wildlife survival and ecological function.

In addition, the concept of *Paseo Pantera* has the potential to catalyze economic growth through ecotourism — tourism oriented toward nature, toward wildlands conservation — with benefits for all countries. The potential for growth in the tourist industry in Central America is based on the assumption that the nearby American public, in addition to more distant populations of Europe and Japan, is ready and eager to travel. We plan to quantitatively test that assumption during the course of our project, but, based on my own experiences, I have a lot of confidence that it's true.

The idea in our project is to foster *regional* travel and, more importantly, regional conservation. We believe a journey through a chain of parks in Central America would be compelling to the traveler. Collectively, the parks of Central America could tell a tale of grand and sweeping themes.

High Jungles and Low serves as a prelude to the exciting project of *Paseo Pantera*. It will whet the appetite to follow the path of the panther from Mexico down to South America, and the traveler will take great delight in sharing Archie's admiration and affection for Central America.

Marjorie Harris Carr
Gainesville, Florida
January 1992

Preface

WHEN I came to put together the bits and pieces that make this book, I failed to find anywhere among them a clue as to how a biology professor with a family came to be living in the rural high tropics. It might be sensed that, being a naturalist, I had always felt a call from the low latitudes; but then lots of people feel that and stay decently at home or maybe assuage the urge with an expedition or two or a conducted tour.

In my case it was more than just the inclination. It was, for instance, the fact that my wife is a naturalist too, between babies. It was also the stacks of T-bone steaks Dr. Popenoe showed me in the school cold room, cut by ebullient students of animal husbandry and awaiting delivery to the faculty; and to my eye, weak from the parsimony of war rationing, an almost obscenely bounteous sight. But what really started me down the path to this odd, pleasant, revolutionary interlude was a letter from Thomas Barbour.

I was working on a book about turtles at the time, and I got bogged down in the sea turtles. I couldn't decide whether the turtles in the eastern Pacific were exactly the same as those in the Atlantic or slightly different. Since museum collections of sea turtles are inadequate, I began to meditate on the possibility of my going down where the oceans are close together to compare their turtles directly.

As was my custom whenever I wanted anything badly, I wrote T. B. He answered promptly: "Go down to Honduras and see Pop. Pop knows everything worth knowing about Central America. While you're there see what you can catch for the museum [the Museum of Comparative Zoology at Harvard] in the pine woods above the School." Since the letter inclosed a check, I hastened to take Dr. Barbour's advice.

"Pop" was Wilson Popenoe, who had just finished building Escuela Agrícola Panamericana for the United Fruit Company in the beautiful high valley of the Yeguare River in the mountains of southern Honduras. The first crop of graduates had just been turned out, the budded mangoes were about to bear, you could get a good horse for twenty-five dollars, and the sun flooded the valley through the most exciting air I had ever breathed. I walked about the palm-grove campus and through the school buildings and brand-new staff residences, all built in gracefully solid colonial style of hand-cut rhyolite from the school quarry, timbered and beamed with Danlí cedar and pine from the mountainside, and roofed with half-round tiles of red school clay. I talked with students from thirteen different countries of tropical America. The frangipanis were blooming and roses were everywhere and the roadside erythrinums were just coming into flame. It was all enough to divert a more constant purpose than mine, and I felt hardly any disappointment at all when Dr. Popenoe turned out to known nothing about sea turtles, because he offered me a job.

I had just wound up a two-year tour in the Army Air Force Pre-Flight Program at the University of Florida, where I taught elementary physics to impatient cadets and dreamed of the time when I could be a naturalist again. I was ripe for Dr. Popenoe's offer. I took it and went home to tell my wife.

She was ready to go before I finished the story. We sold our house, got a three-year leave of absence from the university, and moved south with the faith and fervor of September teal. We took two little children with us, and soon had two more; and part of the fun was seeing them grow up talking Spanish exactly like the cowboys and oxdrivers they revered.

The school gave us a pleasant house and cheerful servants to run it, and we had a strawberry bed and no morning classes and three months out of the year to collect and explore and get to know the tropics. If you wanted horses you sent a note to the head *vaquero*, and your horses turned up in an hour, saddled and tied to a tree beside the house. Every morning posses of students came around to the back of the house — the flower of Indo-American youth at the kitchen door, every one at that marvelous age, so strongly marked in Latins, when lust for the cook exactly balances lust for the cookies she bakes. They came with lists from the dairy and the vegetable garden and the meat-cutting room, and you just checked the vegetables or the amounts of beef and milk and butter you needed; or more shrewdly got the cook to check them.

There was never anything like it. There was plenty of game to shoot and a little-known wilderness at your doorstep. The volcano-set Pacific shore was sixty miles to the south and the hot, lush banana coast a hundred miles to the north; and you could climb a mountain three miles away and find any sort of weather you hankered after.

It was nearly always springtime there in the valley. There were seasons, but mostly they were just different kinds of springtime. The days were golden, and there was a special kind of night that came very often, when the cool air drifted down from the mountains and across the day-warm chaparral, gathering spice all the way, stirring the fireflies in the pastures, and bringing the thin yammer of distant coyotes through the rustling palm crowns. The slow wind raised the curtains at the tall windows and kept you too aware of the world to sleep; but it didn't matter because on nights like that two carpenters got restless, and when the valley lights began to wink out, they came down from the creek on the hillside to serenade — Paco with his guitar and Julio with his velvet voice; and when they sang *El Arriero* under the palms in the yard you heard your wife reflexively clawing the pins from her hair and fumbling for a lipstick in the dark.

Before we went to Honduras I used to wonder why everybody doesn't live between two thousand and four thousand feet above the sea and twenty degrees north and south of the equator. After living there myself for five years and thinking it over in retrospect, and after reading Marston Bates' book *Where Winter Never Comes,* I wonder more than ever if the population of our planet isn't due for a major reshuffling. Maybe life down there wasn't all strawberries and roses, but it's hard now to recollect any other side. Of course, you miss a few of the blandishments of northern cities, but that's true of any rural living. I don't remember ever feeling homesick for the temperate zone as such, but since coming away I've never wavered in my nostalgia for the tropics.

I have promised the publishers that I would say something about the title, *High Jungles and Low*. Their copyright lawyer got uneasy when he learned that William Beebe once wrote a book called *High Jungle*. I will admit that my title sounds like an effort to go Dr. Beebe one better, but it wasn't — at least not a conscious one. Nevertheless we wrote Dr. Beebe with some humility, and he was kind enough to agree that the partial duplication was a trifling matter; and since I like my title very much, we decided to hang on to it.

Just out of curiosity, though, I have been casting about in my cluttered subconscious for some hint as to how the title actually did take shape. If spontaneous generation is ruled out, then maybe Dr. Beebe's *High Jungle was* in on the conception somehow — as one of the gametes, so to speak. But if so, then the other was surely the title of Gordon MacCreagh's *White Waters and Black*. This strange tale affected me strongly back in my adolescent days, and while I had forgotten it completely, the cadence of the title must have been lurking about some place, since mine scans exactly the same.

But there is a limit to a man's liability for the quirks of

his subconscious, and I haven't even bothered to write to MacCreagh's publisher.

I should like to be able to thank all the people who helped me see or do or understand the things this book records, but they are too numerous, and I can only hint at who they were. The list includes a great many of the officials of the United Fruit Company in Central America — not only my colleagues at the school, but a host of others in the divisions from Guatemala to Costa Rica. It includes also a number of other North Americans living in Honduras — especially former personnel of the Rosario and Agua Fría Mining companies — and the sequence of visitors, both gringo and Latin, who came to see Honduras while I was there and roamed the woods with me and helped turn small events into ideas. Later on I incurred wide indebtedness among my friends and associates at the University of Florida for help in preparing the book for publication. Finally, for their contribution to the most stimulating years of my life, I am bound to thank the people of Honduras, whom I greatly admire.

University of Florida   A.C.
March 2, 1953

PART ONE

The Land

The Weeping Woods

As one wanders about the highlands of Honduras and asks people the names of their highest local peaks, the answer comes back, again and again, "La Llorona"; that is to say, La Montaña Llorona, which means "The Weeping Woods." The people thus allude, with characteristic imagery, to the tearlike fall of water that condenses on the trees of the cloud forest. How the word montaña *came to mean woods is another story.*

TOWARD the end of April the high valleys of southern Honduras, which have lain waterless beneath the fierce tropical sun since November, begin to dry up. One can count the boulders in the once lush pastures, and the scant, green carpet has withered under the dusty pines on the mountainsides. The cedars and the stubby-limbed ceibas wait leafless for the rains of June; only the imperturbable mimosas, the coyol palms, and the figs and *guanacastes* along the watercourses relieve the brown monotony. The cows go dry; the steers are skinny and listless and seek shade in preference to the tasteless stubble. At night thin red lines snake along the flanks and summits of the mountains, where ground fires scavenge in the crisp remnants of the pine woods understory. The wind that sporadically sweeps up from the Pacific toward morning is hot, like air from Texas prairies or city asphalt.

Toward the end of April, too, our nerves unravel. We begin to get sick of the *verano,* with its blue haze of smoky dust, and its tough beef, and chronic thirst. Our spirits droop in the heat and drought, and we wonder pettishly if it will ever again be cool and wet. Our bitterness mounts with the realization that we must wait for the rains of June.

But is June really the only way out? How about the 6,300-foot peak of Uyuca that rises at the valley's edge only two miles or so away? And how about Portillo and Monte Crudo and El Volcán? They are all much nearer than June and are cool little isolated worlds, as abruptly disjunct and unexpected — and as welcome — as a palm-shaded well in the Sahara. Up there where the clouds cruise by on the unhindered trade wind, the pine woods give way and the *montaña,* the cloud forest, sucks water from the eternal mists and mocks the forty-inch rainfall of the valley below.

From various points in the valley around Escuela Agrícola Panamericana ten cloud-forested peaks may be seen. A visit to even the nearest of them means a long, hot climb, but the reward is great and the climb itself is interesting. It takes us out of the valley with its chaparral and coyotes into the open pine woods of the surrounding hills, with a very different fauna. A couple of thousand

feet of this parklike *ocotal,* and the ocote pine is replaced
by another species, known locally as *pinabete,* often bur-
dened with epiphytes and sometimes mixing or alternating
with liquidambar, the familiar sweet gum of the southeastern United States. Each of the transition areas between these vertical zones is the equivalent of many miles
of latitude in the faunal and floral changes it brings,
and each tempts the biologist to tarry. But in the drought
of April it is better to climb on, emerging from the *pina-
betal,* crossing the fringing fields and blackberry tangles,
pushing through the second growth *guamil* and passing
at last between the outer columnar trunks of the high
forest. Abruptly, midday changes to owl's-light, and the
dry breeze behind is damped to a slow drift of air that
is eight to ten degrees cooler than that in the valley, and
heavy with moisture and the smell of wet plants.

The cloud-forest community is primeval and self-
perpetuating. As in any mature humid woods, the taller
trees meet above in a continuous leaf-stratum, which
opens only here and there to admit splotches of sunlight.
Competition for light among the numerous species of gigantic oaks and *aguacates* (wild avocados) leaves little
for the plants of the dim understory to fight over, but
tree ferns and spindly palms thrive, varying in relative
abundance from one forest to another and occasionally
attaining heights of thirty feet or more. Giant-leaved wi-
gandias and a purple-flowered fuchsia glean light in the
shadows. The curious tropical melostomes, with a host of
species in the lowland rain forest and a few others in the
dry uplands, here show their versatility in a whole new
series of forms, which range in size from small shrubs to

5

fair-sized trees. The smaller plants are tender, gloom-loving begonias, aroids and peperomias, pteridophytes and mosses in endless variety, lichens, liverworts, and algae, all of which grow equally well on the ground and on the grotesquely buttressed, deeply fluted, and vine-embraced trunks of the older trees.

It is next to impossible to look up and determine with certainty which leaves belong to a particular tree. The confusion of interlacing branches is complete, and a tree which bears, say, three tons of leaves may, according to my reckoning, support five tons of epiphytes ranging in bulk from microscopic algae, tiny mosses, and half-inch orchids to enormous, thick-leaved, woody parasites, one individual of which may replace a third or even half of the original tree-crown. On one eighteen-inch length of tree-fern trunk I was able to find twenty-four species of plants, and I am sure that a botanist would in several cases have distinguished between species that I lumped together. On the drenched and windy peak of El Volcán I climbed a tree that was twisted and wind-pruned like a tree on ocean dunes and that had the usual investment of mosses, selaginellas, and filmy ferns concealing every inch of limb surface. Besides this, it bore four different kinds of leaves in approximately equal abundance, and I would have challenged any botanist to determine which belonged to the original host trunk without making a laborious dissection of the tree.

In the high but protected and relatively level coves and glens, such as the superb Plano Aguacatal in the San Juancito range, or the little hidden plateau where the waters of the Santa Clara arise on the slopes of Monserrat, a number of oaks, *aguacates*, and other trees unknown to me grow to immense size, and the forests surpass in stateliness anything in my experience, except the primeval rain forest of the Caribbean border.

But the dominant plants of the cloud forest are not the giant trees; they are the epiphytes that live on them. The most important factor in the development of these woods is water vapor — not precipitation — and the air-plants, high and low, respond more directly to this influence than those with roots in the ground. If a tree wins out over its neighbors and rises above them, thousands of unbidden guests seek to share its advantage. They pile up in sodden tons on the trunk and branches and crowd the leaves at the tips of the slenderest twigs. During heavy rains the added burden of water they hold is often too much for the great limbs, and they may crash to the ground, ripping out sections of the trunk as they fall. Apparently, the normal ultimate fate of the big cloud-forest trees is to be overcome by epiphytes, insidiously, leaf by leaf, or by catastrophic collapse, or by a combination of the two.

The dominance of the epiphytes is particularly obvious in the exposed levels above sixty-five hundred feet, where the large-leaved trees of the protected places are replaced by heaths, *Podocarpus*, wax myrtle, and other small- and hard-leaved species. It is hard to explain this transition to what looks like an arid-land flora on these high peaks which receive a maximum of water supply through condensation of moisture from the nearly continuous winds, unless it be that the stronger winds augment the hazard in a temporary failure of the moisture supply. These scant-leaved, dwarfed, and wind-tortured trees are often little more than framework for the support of masses of air plants, and a tree that at first glance appears to be alive may be nothing but a corpse, completely enshrouded by the epiphyte flora that killed it.

At seventy-five hundred feet on Peña Blanca in the San Juancito Mountains, the vegetation is a wild, unsorted hodgepodge. There is no distinguishing among limbs, trunks, and roots, for all loop and twist and sprawl about on the steep rock faces beneath a heavy, wet mat of lower plants. Only here and there a plume of leaves projects from the crazy mass to mark the site where a tree reaches for a pittance of light in the face of almost insuperable competition.

A feature of the cloud forests almost as striking as the lavishness of their plant life is their relative poverty in animals — a poverty both in species and in individuals, but most markedly in the latter. Expecting to find a luxuriant environment supporting a dense and varied animal population, one enters the woods prepared to marvel at the fauna. It is entirely possible to wander about for hours, however, and even for days, amid this floral splendor and see only a little more in the way of animals than might be found in a well-kept greenhouse.

To illustrate the sort of jolt that this hothouse sterility delivers to one's preconceptions, consider the case of the bromeliaceous air plants. It would be hard to mention a minor environmental niche that holds, and usually fulfills, more promise for the herpetological collector than these epiphytic, water-storing plants of the pineapple family. In many regions, if a bromeliad can be found, the reward

of from one to a dozen or more specimens is almost auto-
matic. In the dry tropics, the smooth, broad-based leaves
and nearly permanent axillary pools of cool water offer
irresistible quarters for various species of frogs, salamanders, lizards, snakes, insects, and mollusks, and some of
these have become drastically adapted in structure to life
in air plants. These facts are well and widely known, but
to the seasoned collector who, reading this, may find their
repetition tedious I suggest that he go with me to Portillo
de los Arados. Here the forest climbs a sixty-degree slope
from a fern-shaded spring and rill among the rocks to
the tip of a 6,000-foot peak, and the trees bear more
bromeliads· than I ever saw before. Or, rather, I should
say *bore* more bromeliads, because I think we clawed
down half of them in the excitement of our conviction
that here, at last, we would find salamanders on the Pacific slope of Honduras. We hauled them down, one after
another, dumping upon our shivering persons the quart
or gallon of cold water that each contained and finding
not one single vertebrate animal. Of invertebrates there
were only some sow bugs, an occasional centipede, several scorpions (one of which stung me), and swarms of
ants (nearly all of which stung me).

After that, we sulked in the valley for nearly two weeks
and did not go near the high woods.

But this was a mistake. When finally we returned it was
to spend the night in a tiny milpa deep in the forest of
El Volcán. We slept on the ground and were awakened
in the vaporous dawn by the ethereal songs of scores of
jilgueros, the incomparable notes of which express so precisely in fluid sound the spirit of the high forest. We lay

under our tarpaulin watching the heavy white mist drift over us and listening to the ecstatic notes of the unseen birds singing in a cloud, and forgot for good the fiasco of the bromeliads.

Much later, on this same mountain, I had the supreme reward of seeing my first male quetzal. It was five-thirty in the afternoon of a day spent in fruitless search of quetzals. We had scaled the dripping peak of El Volcán, descending it on the opposite side and laboriously working our way back around the base to the homeward trail. As the sun was setting we crossed a little clearing bounded by the towering silvery trunks of the primeval forest. I sat down to spend the few remaining minutes of daylight watching the forest border for anything that might emerge while my companion went to fetch the horses. The brief sunset spread flame through the clouds behind the western ranges, and desultory shreds of mist began to spiral down into the milpa. For once there was almost no wind, and the only sounds were occasional incredibly sweet passages from the *jilgueros* and the low, duotone chant of the Mexican trogon in the depths of the forest. Suddenly a harsh, crackling call came from a tall tree at the edge of the woods. I rose and walked toward the tree while the call continued. As I approached, several green toucanets emerged from the tree and flew off over the milpa, pushing their banana-like beaks before them. The raucous cackle continued. Then three quetzals, a female and two gorgeous males, rose above the crown of the tree. One of the males and the female flew directly into the woods, but the other flew and hopped from one tree to another, dashing out of the tree and back, making vertical sallies into the air above and descending again in a wholly uncalled-for series of swoops and dips and pirouettes to display his crimson breast, the blue-green fire of his wings, and the grace of his yard-long tail. This was reward enough, and indeed if the forest grew for no other end than to support this bird it were no waste.

There is a handful of animals that a quiet observer may see on nearly any given visit to one of the local cloud forests. These creatures are for the most part species peculiar to montane communities and with wide but necessarily discontinuous distribution throughout Central America. Like most habitués of deep forests, they know how to live inconspicuously in the background of their environment.

If you want to see them you will have to sit on a log and wait. If your log lies at the edge of a clearing you will almost immediately see on a nearby stump a big green or sooty-black fence lizard of the genus *Sceloporus*. If the time is early morning or late afternoon, or if the clouds are drifting through the forest on a gentle wind, you will not wait long for the songs of the *jilguero*, or nightingale thrush, and the black robin, known here as *sinzontle*. Both are skilled ventriloquists, and, though they may sound their flutelike arpeggios from no more than a few yards away, they are very hard to see. Long before you locate a singer a flock of clorospingas will pass by in the lower trees, squeaking as they hop from one berry-bearing twig to another. If you continue to give no offense a slim brown wood hewer will swoop down to a nearby tree, and stay to chip and poke at the bark and keep an eye on you.

A slender anole will scurry along a vine and stop to spread its orange throat fan; or to nap for a moment in a splash of sunlight, with arms tucked in and legs pressed back against its tail; or perhaps to creep up with horrid stealth and seize a simple-minded crane fly. A small, short-eared squirrel that has been looking at you in silence for a long time will suddenly materialize, often under your very nose, and try to scold without dropping the avocado that it holds in its mouth.

Sooner or later you will become aware of a tiny, intricate song, sung in an excited whisper somewhere close by. This is Rehn's mountain wren, through some ornithologist's whimsey, and when you finally locate the red-brown dwarf it will have been nearly within reach of your hand all the while.

The robin chirp of the dusky *zorzal* is never long still. Usually the woods echo also with one or both of two other bird calls — one the monotonous and incessant single note of the white-faced quail dove, and the other the brooding chant of the Mexican trogon.

Among the few actually conspicuous inhabitants of the cloud forests are the hummingbirds when they are in season. They are of a dozen or more species, and to the eye accustomed only to the common rubythroat of the United States their variety in size and coloration is striking. They range from tiny mites noticeably smaller than the rubythroat up to a glossy dark species with a body the size of a man's big finger. During September and October, when the wild *aguacates* bloom and the melostomes and vacciniums strew the ground with shed corollas, the hummingbirds leave the fields and *guamil* and blackberry tangles and move into the depths of the forest in hordes. They suck the high blossoms and make their perfect little nests of live moss covered with lichens and lined with the silken fiber of the tree fern. Their voices are as various as their shapes and sizes, and the males scold and squabble incessantly. One misanthropic species marks the course of any intruder who walks through the woods by repeatedly taking stations on twigs just in front of him and uttering raucous cheeps in outraged monotone, once a second without ceasing until the trespasser has crossed the bounds of what the bird regards as his rightful freehold. Another species vents its seemingly chronic indignation by zigzagging angrily among the trees around the human visitor, often diving at his head at breakneck speed, and all the while rattling out a querulous complaint for all the world like a midget kingfisher. Among themselves they fight bitterly and often, and their quarrels are both intra- and interspecific without bias. If you lie on your back and stare upward at the level where the treetops interlace high above, you may see pairs of buglike hummingbirds zipping over and under the green canopy like dogfighting planes diving into and out of cloud banks. One such pair may suddenly plunge downward in a breathless spiral, the hind bird following in machine-like detail every intricacy of the mad course of the pursued. They collide in mid-air in front of your face with what ought to be crushing force and then fly separately away to sit on twigs and preen and await the fine new surge of anger that will tune their incredible little muscles for more joyous combat.

Hummingbirds are birds apart. They are miracles of

mechanical design and physiologic efficiency. Their initiative and courage are beyond reproach, and in many species the splendor of their coloring can hardly be matched in the biologic world. But few who know them will go much further in their praise. For the rest, they are peevish and generally ornery and are no comfort either to themselves or to anyone who lives with them.

Of invertebrate animals the most noteworthy — in its abundance as well as in the incongruity of its occurrence on a mountain peak — is a crab. To me, a crab has no business in fresh water and much less in a cloud forest, and I still feel an irrational sort of skepticism every time I see one. The small, black mountain species lives in the beds and borders of foaming creeks and rills and around the nearby springs. There it digs caves under rocks where salamanders should be and heaps up mud pellets as crayfish should.

Perhaps of just as much consequence in the forest community as any animal I have mentioned are the several kinds of mice and at least two species of shrews that live underground in the root mazes, but they are almost never seen unless trapped. It is also easy to miss the glistening, yellow-speckled, plated lizard that hunts sow bugs and wolf spiders and spindly-legged crickets in the leaf mold.

Besides the few common and characteristic denizens that one can count on meeting on almost any trip into the *montaña*, there is a long list of creatures which are seen only sporadically, or very locally, or perhaps not at all, and which the forest holds in reserve to shock the observer out of any growing smugness over the authority of his lore. Thus, only one time, after hundreds of hours of observation, did we encounter an anteater, and on the same day we collected our first and only *pava* — the big, burro-voiced *Penelope* — when we walked up under a pair eating berries in a tree at Rancho Quemado. We had hunted deer and frogs on Uyuca so many nights that when finally our lights struck red fire from eyes in the trail ahead we merely stared stupidly as a puma loped slowly up into the darkness and *guamil* above. These animals of rare occurrence not only lend the promise of drama to every collecting trip, but the very eccentricity of their distribution may present problems of irresistible interest to the zoologist.

For example, consider the faunal vagary to be seen in the colony of giant pocket gophers on a mountain in El Paraíso known as Portillo de los Arados. Here the forest has been skinned back on all the slopes up to the sheer crest, which is crowned by what the local mountaineers call a *faja de montaña,* a long narrow strip of well-developed cloud forest. In the margins of this woods and in the milpas that skirt it, the ground is honeycombed by the burrows of an enormous pocket gopher, which we saw on two occasions but never succeeded in collecting. Neither the soil nor the vegetation of this mountain shows any notable difference from those of other mountains that we have visited. The only place in Honduras where pocket gophers are known is Alto Cantoral, north of Tegucigalpa, which is the type locality and only known range of the Honduranean pocket gopher. This is probably the same animal that occurs on Portillo. It seems unlikely that we have merely missed them elsewhere, since their excavations and mounds are very conspicuous and would be next to impossible to overlook. Whether Portillo furnishes the gophers with some vital necessity that is wanting on the other peaks, or whether their restricted distribution reflects instead some event in the history of the region or of the race, is an intriguing question.

Another case of interest is that of the quetzal. This incomparable trogon is a characteristic inhabitant of cloud forests from southern Mexico to Panama. Because of its superb plumage it has been persecuted unmercifully in many places, and its scarcity in suitable areas around the larger towns is probably due chiefly to the work of hunters. But in the rural, south-central part of Honduras, where our series of cloud forests is located, guns are scarce and where found are usually muzzle-loaded with black powder and a quarter-inch cube of bar lead. They are not often used for shooting at birds and even less frequently for killing them.

It seems probable that here the infrequent occurrence of quetzals is due more to the restricted extent of the individual forests than to the killing of birds by hunters. At San Juancito there is far more hunting than in any of the other local forests, and yet the quetzals hold on within sound of blasting at the Rosario mine, because the woods there are almost unbroken over thousands of acres. Likewise, we found quetzals in the Yuscarán Range around El Volcán even though the fifteen to twenty square miles of cloud forest there are spotted with *ranchos* and dissected by cultivation. In the smaller forests, however, such as Montañuela, Portillo, and Monte Crudo, although the physiognomy of the habitat is identical, quetzals are entirely unknown.

In this case the limiting factor would appear to be food. Quetzal existence apparently depends upon a continuous abundance of small fruits. There is evidently an areal threshold below which a given forest is too small to yield these fruits in perennial supply. The birds venture from their primeval habitat far enough to augment their diet with the luscious blackberries that abound in the marginal tangles (as do also the peccaries and, where found, the mountain tapir), but they evidently never migrate and are actually prisoners in their cloud-swept jungles. If the fruit crop fails for a single week they must starve.

Of equal interest, zoologically if not aesthetically, is the *tamagás* of San Juancito. The *tamagás* is a short, fat, irritable viper of the notorious genus *Bothrops*, which includes the *barba amarilla* (fer-de-lance), the horrendous bushmaster, and a host of smaller poisonous snakes. The curious thing about the *tamagás* is that the only ones we ever saw were at Rancho Quemado in the San Juancito Mountains, where they are quite common. In the places where the sun filters down through a break in the tall canopy overhead, they lie around on the leaf mold, their brown and gray color tones and rough scales making them as inconspicuous as mounds of leaves.

We visited Rancho Quemado eight times and only twice failed to see *tamagás*. Al Chable found four in one morning, and fifteen minutes after I had warned Margaret Hogaboom to watch where she put her feet, she stumbled over a *tamagás* in the trail. I collected in Honduras for nearly five years, and the *tamagás* of this colony are the only snakes in the central part of the republic that I should call common. Only here, for instance, would I dare predict that on a given afternoon a snake-collecting jaunt would yield something.

The question of what attraction Rancho Quemado holds for *tamagás* is no great mystery. It gives them deer mice in abundance and an endless system of galleries and intricate moss-lined catacombs beneath the prop and buttress roots of the forest trees. Here they can prowl and forage in comfort when the blood-thickening fog is down and the icy drip turns *tamagás* bodies to rolls of helpless clay. The mice and the catacombs make for what would appear to be an ideal viper environment, and the *tamagás* respond with enthusiasm. Why, then, have we looked in vain for snakes of any kind in identically tunneled and mouse-filled areas in all the other forests?

I believe I know why the *tamagás* do not occur on the other peaks. I think peccaries make life impossible for them. The collared peccaries are ubiquitous despoilers of the cloud forests. We found their tracks or their dung or the wreckage they leave behind in nearly all the forests of the area. They live in the dense *guamiles*, preferably in the ghastly *morales*, or nearly pure stands of giant blackberry bushes, which fringe all the high woods; and here the pigs are safe from molestation by man or beast. Part of the time the bands stay in the margins and eat blackberries, but often they come out to make forays into the milpas below or into the forest above. They are keen and apparently omnivorous foragers, and I imagine that very little that is conceivably edible escapes their jaws. I would not give two cents for the chances of a fat and succulent viper, stupid from overeating or torpid from cold.

Since the pigs do not dwell in the depths of the woods, but rather in the blackberry tangles at the edges, the snake population of a large unbroken tract of forest like San Juancito is practically insulated from the ravages of the peccaries. On all the other mountains, however, the ratio of cutover fringe to virgin *montaña* is so much higher that no section of the woods escapes the sporadic patrols, and snakes cannot survive.

To me, the most curious anomaly of all is the mountain tapir. The mammalogists mostly recognize only one species of tapir in Honduras and so would have us believe that it is one and the same beast that wallows in the creeks of the coastal jungles and scampers about the crags of Chile Mountain. This may be so, but if it is I know of no more impressive example of ecologic tolerance and the broad, flexible outlook. I lived for a month on intimate terms with tapirs in the Nicaraguan rain forest and feel that I know something of their character and aspirations. I cannot believe that the tapir there is the animal that makes the tracks and trails on sheer cliffs of 6,500-foot Pico de Navaja, or ambles about the subalpine *morales* of Batea, picking blackberries, or that ran six miles along the knife-edged ridge of Cerro Brujo to elude completely a gang of mountain-bred dogs. How could the semi-aquatic monster of the Huahuashan swamps slake his chronic thirst or cool his hide on the streamless ridges of Bramadero? I don't believe he does; I think it is a different creature and shall cite one minor aspect of jungle tapir personality to support my stand.

A lowland tapir descends the slopes of ravine side or river bluff in a manner wholly his own and altogether

19

irresponsible. If he arrives at such a declivity at all pressed for time he merely lets go and falls down. His legs move and usually manage to keep him right side up, but they in no way retard the acceleration of gravity. I have seen and heard this phenomenon several times and each time I marveled that the tapir failed to kill himself. On Chile Mountain he would have killed himself. We climbed tapir trails there which required more from the arms than from the legs, and which would demand caution from a mountain goat. Any tapir trying to save time on these trails by falling down them would wind up in the vicinity of Cantarranas, some four thousand feet below and eight miles to the westward.

A comparison of adequate series of specimens of tapirs from the mountains and lowlands seems to me very much in order, and I strongly suspect that when made it will show at least racial differences between the two populations.

As a biotic environment the Honduranean cloud forests offer the biologist a challenge and promise of reward that would be hard to duplicate. But more than this, they hold an infallible aesthetic appeal that is as deep as the mystery of the dim, green woods and as varied as its changing aspects.

One evening we wandered into a grove of *aguacates* up in the San Juancito Mountains above La Tigra. It was in a little glenlike valley just under the summit ridge at sixty-four hundred feet. Interspersed in the curiously homogeneous stand of *aguacates* there were a few enormous, cactus-draped oaks, some of them eight feet through above the fluted buttresses, and a superb understory of tall tree ferns. An acre or more of the flat valley floor was strewn with fragments of partly eaten *aguacate* seeds, presumably left mostly by squirrels. Thinking that the seed-littered glen might be visited after dark by some nocturnal gleaner of interest, we returned to the place at ten o'clock on a windy night. We saw no animals, but we found the forest in a different mood. The moon was full and the big clouds of the Caribbean train were rolling over the ridge on a strong northeast wind. As the dense masses of vapor moved over the glen the moonlight waxed and waned with the fast-changing texture of the cloud field. One moment we could look out over the shimmering stratum of tree-fern tops to the straight white boles of the trees on the far side of the valley. Then the light would fail, and we would stand in the blackness listening to the high, tense hum of the wind as it swept over the crest and through the crowns of the trees.

On the valley floor we were well in the lee of the ridge and felt no wind. Detached jags and streamers of cloud sank among the tree trunks and drifted slowly about or swirled upward in local eddies. For a long time we waited, losing at length all notion of what we waited for. We watched and listened until the enchantment of the place crept into us and we kept vigil no more for anteaters and kinkajous but peered instead after the impossible creatures more appropriate to the setting.

But there was no wingbeat of pterosaur to consummate our suspense. There was only the sound of the wind above and the slow, incessant drip of the cloud-water that had built the forest, the weeping woods, as it fell from the trees that owed their existence to it.

High Jungles and Low

WHEN people speak of the luxuriant animal and plant life of the tropics they may be talking about two very different things. One of these is the classic exuberance of life in a single extraordinary tropical community — the lowland rain forest; and the other is the zoogeographic diversity that comes with a strong topographic relief in a warm, most region.

The most impressively rich environment in the tropics is the evenly hot, wet rain forest, in each acre of which productivity may be higher and more energy tied up in animal and plant protoplasm than anywhere, except perhaps in lakes and seas. When to this varied and abundant life is added the gamut of faunas and floras that accompany a deeply broken topography, the total varietal richness of the region may represent a maximum for the whole earth.

For obvious reasons strong relief usually produces a

greater variety of physical conditions in the tropics than in temperate latitudes. The graded fall in temperature, with increasing elevations, for instance, gives the life-space a third dimension and, operating both directly and jointly with humidity, stratifies the fauna and flora, and augments the multiplicity in the lowland selva with wholly new elements. In Central America northern animals and plants tend to follow temperature belts as far southward as the altitudes allow them to exist, and it is thus not surprising to find a steady increase in the northern flavor of the biota as one ascends a mountain from the coastal plain.

Besides the layering of faunas and floras according to temperature, there are in the mountainous tropics moisture zones that either correspond roughly with the temperature belts or, more often, cut across or are completely independent of them. Where the trade winds predominate, the windward slopes of mountain ranges may take most of the available water out of the clouds that cross the land. The incoming clouds rise with the slope, expand as they rise, and cool as they expand. The cooling condenses the vapor, and it falls as rain on the slopes the cloud is hurdling.

Where the windward ranges are very high the even increase in this so-called orographic rainfall may not continue on up to the crest. The upsurge of air induced by the climbing drive of the wind combines with convection currents from the sun-heated land to boost the clouds upward at an angle much steeper than the slope of the land. The line of maximum rainfall may then be far to windward of the crests, and perhaps no higher than a thousand feet or even less on the exposed slopes. From here upward, rainfall decreases and the highest summits may get very little real rain; yet they may be bathed almost constantly in the thin mists of the dried-out sea-clouds that drag their fringes across them.

Going down the off side of the mountain the mist-bath rapidly fails, and the lower flanks and lee approaches are dry steppe, or desert. They lie in what is sometimes called a "rain shadow." From the barrier ranges on back across the country there is increasingly less orographic rain, and it rains at all only when seasonal changes in the noon position of the sun shift the positions of the air masses from which the weather comes; or when a cold front bulges down from the north, ploughs under the warm country air, and causes the files of rain storms called line squalls.

When strong differences in altitude are squeezed into a narrow area the interplay of these factors, and of a host of others of lesser but still conspicuous importance, can mold a biota so varied in the aggregate that it overshadows even the rank redundance of its lowland component.

In the narrow Middle American isthmus conditions are ideal to exploit the potentialities of the latitude. High mountains rise abruptly from steaming lowlands, blocking the sweep of a steady planetary wind that pushes the big Caribbean clouds over the rising land, where they climb and spill their rain and grow to be towers of white and gray vapor, and then cruise on into the land and toward the Pacific beyond it. This basic relationship of climate to topography allows the endless combinations of altitude and exposure to produce a bewildering array of environments, and some of these are so drastically different that one might expect to have to go a thousand

miles to reach one from the other. These numerous sub-
environments or "habitats," and the animals and plants
that live in them, may be grouped into four or five big com-
plexes called life zones, or perhaps better, biotic provinces,
all of which overlap to some extent or merge and give
way to one another in all sorts of ways, but which maintain their identity on the average and are sometimes very
clearcut indeed. Thus, in northern Honduras it is not hard
to find a high point from which an observer can see in
one panoramic view territory in all the four life areas that
occur in the country. Moreover, it is often possible to dis-
tinguish these areas from a great distance by the gross
features of their vegetation; but it is only a closer inspection that will give any real notion of the scope of the thing
one is seeing.

A logical place to begin a quick transect of the Honduranean life areas is the Caribbean lowland where the
climate-breeding trade wind enters. Here in the coastal
plain and on the northern slopes of the coastal mountains, the annual rainfall ranges well over eighty inches
(up to more than two hundred fifty a short distance to
the south), and the dry season is half-hearted. These are,
in the conventional sense of the word, the real "tropics"
where, except for man's clearings, the selvas, jungles, savannas, and monsoon forests extend unbroken from Mexico to Brazil, and are roamed by much the same fauna
throughout.

The salient characteristic of the rain-forest vegetation
is the almost infinite variety of the plants that compose
it. Only rarely do the trees assemble themselves in ex-
clusive bands of a single species, but rather they shun

their own kind and seek isolation in heterogeneous crowds of alien kinds. This tendency is so marked among some of the important economic species, such as mahogany, that a population of one mature tree per acre is regarded by the trade as a valuable stand; and the *hulero* (the rubber cutter) is forced to cruise a most unbelievably broad territory to locate enough mature *hule* trees to establish a profitable line.

In written accounts of tropical jungles much use is made of such feverish adjectives as "riotous," "profligate," "teeming," "tumultuous," and the like. I probably have used some of them myself in this chapter. But actually these words are not at all appropriate for describing, even in a figurative sense, the interior of the primeval *selva*, the so-called "climax" rain forest. Only when the structure of the forest has been shattered does it show the confusion and disarray implied in all these terms. If lightning kills a big tree, or if men make and abandon a clearing, the sudden flood of light lets loose all the wild capacity for growth that has lain quiet in the relentless shade of the mature woods. There is chaos for a time as the light-frenzied pioneer plants fight and scramble over one another and fill the new space with formless disorder. But this is only temporary. If left to itself the melee under the torn canopy will burn itself out and the architecture of maturity will slowly be restored as the climax plants move back in, sort themselves out, and take their respective positions and levels; and when one walks through the fully rebuilt forest the adjectives that come to mind are "serene," "majestic," "ordered," or even "austere."

The interior of the *selva* is open below and many-layered above, where the tree-crowns form three, four, or five canopies, one spread above the other and together permitting no precious ray of direct sunlight to spill itself upon the ground. The trunks of the trees are usually smooth and light colored, and many of them are strongly buttressed at the base. The trees of the top canopy, and the 200-foot giants standing shoulder-high above it, are mostly small-leaved; those of the light-hungry lower levels are often big-leaved, and in the twilight understory many of the soft-stemmed herbs and shrubs have immense leaves with glossy surfaces that pass the dilute light back and forth as if to share the last of it with their fellows. Vines and creepers tie the high limbs together and huge lianas drop to the ground from the green ceiling. Epiphytes — orchids, bromeliads, ferns, and mosses — are well represented but are not nearly so profuse in either kinds or mass as in the high cloud forests.

The clean rise of the pale tree trunks from the fluted slopes of their spread bases, together with the long aisles and vistas and the plunge of the liana-ropes from the green glow of the high domes down into the half-light of the understory, give the interior of the selva a spacious Gothic dignity not quite matched by any other forest.

The rain-forest animals too are varied, although unevenly distributed and nowhere equaling the multiform luxuriance of the flora. Moreover, they often show a stubborn tendency to keep out of sight that has brought bitter frustration to many a zoologist. The cats — ocelot, puma, and jaguar — are masters at eluding observation. A puma, or *león*, as he is called in Latin America, will lie motionless between the buttresses of a great tree and watch a machete crew slash a *piquete* only a few yards away. Elsewhere I have told of the jaguar that walked, unseen as a ghost, for miles between me and the next man only a few minutes ahead of me on the trail. For all its ungainly bulk the tapir too is seldom seen, and one may live a long time with paca, *sajino*, brocket, and sloth and see only circumstantial evidence of their presence. The black magic by which a hunter may suddenly find himself surrounded by a whole sea of cruising *wari*, or white-lipped peccaries, is unsettling when he recalls their reputation as the only really dangerous mammal in tropical America.

In contrast to the more retiring forest animals are the coatis, high-tailed and blasé, the kinkajous that whistle as they play and fight in the treetops at night, and above all the irrepressible, extroverted monkeys. An irate band of capuchins will move in to close quarters to throw down litter and abuse at a passing party; and howler monkeys may lounge and sprawl about on overhanging limbs to watch for idle hours on end the activities of a camp below. Spider monkeys are clowns and exhibitionists and frequently engage in the most exuberant acrobatics just to prove the virtuosity of their super-prehensile tails. After dark they tell of their presence in a different mood, when they may croak and shriek for half the night after a jaguar or a puma has passed beneath their bed-tree.

As much a part of the selva as the trees are its bird voices. Wherever the proper fruits grow the parrots and macaws gather and mingle their outrageous cries with the percussive outbursts of oropendulas, the creaking of toucans, and the booming of pigeons. Along the ravines motmots hoot and trogons chant their brooding notes. On the ridges where the understory is clear the *pavones* — the big, turkey-like curassows — voice their bull-fiddle call, and in the palm jungles the sudden hysterical bray of the smaller *pava* greets the intruder. At dawn and dusk, and sometimes in the dead of night, two extraordinary voices call — one the cacophonic shouting of a big, ornate forest quail; the other the eerie and surpassingly lovely cry of the tinamou. Besides these there are myriad smaller voices — some unimpressive, some inexpressibly melodious — which only an ornithologist could name, and I suspect that even he would often be hard pressed.

During the short dry season the really heavy rain forest — the tall selva — is an extremely pleasant place. The temperature is even and never too high for comfort. Mosquitoes and other biting insects are rarely a nuisance. Ticks may occur, but never so abundantly as in drier and more open country, and the same may be said for poisonous snakes.

There is so much of interest in the rain forest that one hesitates to leave it for the inhospitable drought in the semi-deserts that lie behind the coastal ranges, and in rain shadows generally throughout the interior. But our aim is a speaking acquaintance with all the life areas, and before we can again wander in tall timber — next time in the cloud forests on the distant peaks that rise into the Humid Upper Tropical Zone — we must traverse the Arid Lower Tropical of the inland valleys and the Arid Upper Tropical with its widespread mountain-slope pine woods, or *ocotal*.

In the Arid Lower Tropical valleys, where annual rainfall averages between twenty and forty inches and comes mostly in a few torrential rains between May and October, we find a prairie-land fauna — although still with a low-land tropical tinge most noticeable near the larger water courses. The vegetation includes a variety of dry-land communities in which cactus, agave, acacia, mimosa, and other common thorn-forest plants occur. Coyotes howl at night, and other common larger mammals are foxes, skunks, deer, and armadillos, which contribute to the impression that you are somewhere, say, along the Rio Grande in northern Mexico. Then you run across a por-cupine or an anteater, and don't know where you are. Caracaras and sun bitterns stalk across the recent burns eating roasted grasshoppers, and the more conspicuous snakes are rattlesnakes, whip snakes, and gopher snakes, while the commoner lizards are race runners and fence lizards. For the rest, the reptile fauna spends most of its time underground in burrows of tarantulas, armadillos, or leaf-cutting ants, and most of the frogs, likewise, live chiefly in holes in the baked earth.

On the sharper slopes at the valley edges the pine zone begins. The pine of the lower levels is the ocote (*Pinus oocarpa*), which grows in open stands on soil that may be so scant as to leave bare large areas of bedrock. In the *ocotal*, which is the most widespread vegetation type in the Arid Upper Tropical Zone, there is a decided increase in the northern faunal element, and many of the tropical forms found in the valleys below drop out. The bobwhite call of the valley quail is rarely heard here, where instead, small coveys of big mountain partridges stuff themselves with the pseudobulbs of tiny ground orchids that they scratch from the gravelly soil. The bizarrely crested magpie jay of the valley is replaced by the smaller but equally noisy Steller's jay of deep metallic blue plumage. The road runner, called here, unaccountably, *alma de perro*, or "soul of a dog," scuttles across the trail. Bluebirds are abundant, the ivory-billed woodpecker chops on the dead trunks, and crossbills putter among the pine cones.

At about four thousand feet the underbrush becomes noticeably heavier and air plants begin to perch on the pine limbs. At levels varying between four and five thousand feet a different pine (*Pinus pseudostrobus*) appears. Known locally as *pinabete*, its needles are lighter green and more feathery than those of the ocote below, and its wood is a magnificent timber similar to white pine. The higher humidity here permits the development of a profuse aerial flora of orchids and bromeliads that envelop the limbs and trunks of the trees, at times almost concealing them.

Where the water table stands high the forest of *pinabete* may be invaded or even replaced entirely by liquidambar, the familiar and beautiful sweet gum so common in the hammocks of the southeastern United States. By some odd, and to me unexplained, etymological twist, this tree has no local Indian name but is known instead as *liquidumbe*, *liquidambe*, or *diquidumbe*, all obviously modifications of the term on which the generic botanical name was based.

Under ideal conditions, which seem to include, besides available ground water, a more level terrain than pine thrives on and protection from wind, these stands of sweet gums form elegant groves, and the trees far exceed in size anything I ever saw in Florida. We found one such forest on the eastern flank of the Guaimaca Range where the hundred-foot trees were regularly three and four, and occasionally as much as five, feet thick above the buttress. The symmetrical trunks rose clean sixty feet without a limb, some stark white like stone, some spirally wound with climbing arums. It was curious and somewhat eerie to find trees that should have been old friends in such a strange community. Although we knew well the tears of fragrant balsam and the deep-toothed leaves and prickly, spherical fruit on the ground, there was nothing familiar in the continuous, towering canopy or in the mid-day twilight beneath it, or in the stately columns that marched out evenly through the gloom like half-authentic sweet gums of a dream.

In a sense this high woods of pine and sweet gum represents the beginning of the cloud forest, since it is here that a conspicuous epiphytic flora, sustained directly by atmospheric moisture, appears. Here the big valley squirrel and the rat-sized one of the summit cloud forest meet, and the mountain quail reaches maximum abundance. Ravens nest and croak in the tall *pinabetes*, and the new visitor is shocked by the maniacal clamor of the black chachalaca, which somewhere on the slopes below took over from its smaller lowland relative. The same gopher snake that occurs in the valley is met here with greater frequency, and the commonest reptile is a big, rough-scaled fence lizard which ranges in color from sooty to lettuce green and which has never been seen in the valleys. The burred breeding trill of the marine toad is not heard here; the July ravines ring instead with the sweet trilling whistle of *Bufo coccifer*, and three tree frogs un-

known below call in the tumbling *quebradas* or from tus-
socks in the high, flat bogs.

Except on the steepest and wholly untillable cliff-faces
the pine-liquidambar level is margined above by fields or
second growth which mark the original lower extensions
of the cloud forest and which may be found in all stages
of reversion toward it. To the gringo acquainted from
childhood with Appalachian meadows in the springtime
these high fields have a nostalgic appeal that is poignant
but hard to define. I think it is mostly the hot sun through
the high, cool air and a chance compounding of the smell
of ripe blackberries and guavas and the color of ageratums
and the sighing song of the gold-finches. In season her-
baceous wildflowers are more abundant here than at any
other level. Two species of *Salvia* — one Indian red, the
other royal blue — and an orange-yellow composite like a
small sunflower are often nearly equally represented in
dense, waist-high stands; and, where protected from the
wind, these trifloral crazy-quilts spread unbroken up the
sharp slopes in a dazzling show of discordant color.

Beyond the fields and marginal tangles of briers and
saplings rises the cloud forest, the *montaña llorona*, the
characteristic plant community of the Humid Upper Tropical, and one of the world's great displays of vegetable
luxuriance.

Although superficially similar — in their cool, submarine
gloom and in the immense size of their trees — cloud forest and rain forest are on closer inspection very different.
The trees of the cloud forest are not only wholly different
species but are of a mere handful of kinds compared to
the almost endless variety of the rain-forest flora. In Hon-

duras, Nicaragua, and Costa Rica perhaps 75 per cent of the cloud-forest trees may be either oaks of a number of kinds, or *aguacates* and closely related lauraceous species. On the other hand, the rain-fed selva cannot begin to match the riotous profusion of the cloud-forest epiphytes.

One of the most striking differences is the extraordinary meagerness of the cloud-forest fauna. Though of the greatest zoogeographic interest because it is discontinuously distributed in islands of humid woods separated by steppe or desert terrain, and though it includes such unique creatures as the jeweled quetzal and the little gray *jilguero* with the bewitching, honey-gold voice that must have few rivals in the world, this is nevertheless a remarkably poor fauna.

It is so dilute, in fact, that the uninitiated zoologist tends to lay the dearth of animals to deficiency in his own power of observation. Such a conclusion has been made easy for him by the many writers on tropical natural history who have marvelled at the secretiveness of jungle animals. But that is something different. I am fully aware that there are more inept watchers of wild things than good ones, that skill in this line requires endless patience and practice, and that forest beasts may show almost unbelievable capacity for self-effacement. Nevertheless, I am convinced that the faunal poverty of the cloud forests is no illusion. It is a curious, at times bewildering, but very real condition which remains almost entirely unexplained and which is in itself an intriguing problem.

In spite of their marked and fundamental differences in origin, water economy, and botanic composition, the high cloud forest and the coastal selva both have a power to fascinate any but the most workaday of minds with the sheer fecundity of their vegetation and the cool, calm spaciousness of their interiors. And so it is that any naturalist worth his salt — and blessed with the opportunity — will go back day after day to the weeping woods or the rain-fed selva alike, and wander through the dim green light they share, conditioned by the prehuman look of the draped and festooned corridors to face any strange beast whatever, but not really disappointed if he should see nothing but the forest.

The Wasting Land

IT is no longer stylish to talk about inter-American good will. The wartime vogue is gone; the phrase "Good Neighbor" sounds as passé as "P-40" or "Rubber Reserve"; the whole field is back in the hands of people who speak of what they're after as "Hemispheric Solidarity," and no idea with a name like that could ever have any popular appeal. Most inter-American good-will overtures are today promoted under Point Four, and hardly anybody even knows what that means.

That is to say, the question of how we can build and keep the confidence and support of our Latin neighbors has once more become an academic one for most North Americans, with even a taint of the visionary about it. This seems to me a dangerous state of mind to be in. It means that we shall probably go on fumbling our opportunities and alienating people who might someday help us save our half of the world. This bothers only a few

Americans at home, but to those who see our blunders down where they are made, it seems tragic. It bothered me for five years, and I made up my mind that someday I would complain about it and now I am going to do it.

I saw Central America from two quite divergent points of view. My interest in natural history took me away from the cities and out into the back country, where public opinion is born but not often canvassed. I wandered about among the country people, eating their *tortillas* and beans, contracting their parasites, seeing their despair — moving among them with no axe to grind, predisposed to like them, and in my interest in their land and its varmints predisposing them to like me. Time and again my wife and I stopped at some lonely *aldea* to tie our horses before a mud-floored inn, and over coffee and *pan dulce* talk with the *dueño* about Honduras and its chances for a better future.

Back at the school we were at a crossroads of inter-Americanism. The staff and student body were a cross section of Caribbean America and there was a steady stream of visitors, most of them in the field for some international agency, or fired with private schemes for saving or seducing Indo-America.

The war was on, and funds for buying the favor of our neighbors flowed freely. Projects to court the people with the promise of technical or agricultural enlightenment sprouted like mushrooms. Sixteen-hand Missouri mules were brought in to bog down in fields where only oxen could plow, or to pull shiny new red-and-green farm wagons and smash their wheels on roads that only oxcarts could travel. New corn that yielded triply but made bitter *tortillas* was urged upon the Indians, and blooded live-stock of all kinds was brought in to languish and waste away in the face of unforeseen factors like the drought or the rainy season, or the dog days or the altitude, or from peculiar localized agents such as screw worms, *tórsolas,* vampire bats, spider bites, abnormally dense tick populations, or the *comelengua.**

In those days there were coordinators in the land, co-ordinating every imaginable phase of Central American life and leaving their stamp in the shape of a wide-spread neologism, an *hondureñismo* that in the most remote places has come to be used for "a well-intentioned but blundering and impractical fellow." The word is *coordinador.*

These things made a strong impression on me. Now there is evidence that we really learned little from the mistakes we made and that in our anxiety over a restless world we are heading down the same old trails; and I am moved to add a lay voice to the sadly small clamor for more common sense in our inter-American policy and to list the following seven things I think we should do, for the sake of self-preservation, if for no other reason.

1

Improve the quality of the personnel we send to the tropics, especially of agents and specialists who come in

---

*When a steer starves to death in the Honduranean dry season the coyotes and dogs come and pull out its tongue and eat it. The ranchers all say the *comelengua* (tongue-eater) killed the steer. Everybody with any sense believes in the *comelengua.* My friend Joche Midence saw one. It was in the rockfield below Chagüite. It had the body of a short, thick snake, the wings of a buzzard, and the face of a puma. I don't know that the *comelengua* was ever really cited in an agricultural project report as a cause of loss, but it should have been.

contact with the public. In addition to a sound grasp of his specialty and fluency in Spanish, the prospective field man should understand something of the fundamental physical and biological features and problems of the terrain, as well as of the cultural and historical background of the country in which he will work.

2

Stop underestimating the intelligence and sensitivity of the rural Latin American people. The distinction between ignorance and stupidity, between lack of advantage and lack of capacity, has been repeatedly overlooked in our dealings with peons, not only in our commercial contacts but in our often abortive or misunderstood attempts to help them. They are not easy to fool. They see insincerity and impracticality in our dealings with unsettling clarity, and our blunders are not forgotten except by us. Actually, it would be next to impossible for the people to forget them, what with the monuments that stand — the skeletons of all the fancy projects that fizzled out for lack of a background of sound reconnaissance. The millions of dollars that these bone piles cost us were not just thrown away. They brought a good measure of ridicule and mistrust, which in many places now stands as a wall between our propaganda and the people it would persuade.

A barefoot *arriero* whom I maneuvered into frank comment on the ruins of one of our wartime demonstration projects wound up his appraisal something like this:

"If the gringos want to spend money to make us like them why don't they spend it on something that will really help us?"

I was glad the question was rhetorical, because it was too much for me to answer.

3

Avoid irresponsible spending for unnecessary technical assistance. Design technical aid programs that will improve the economic level of the people – not just of the men who govern them or employ them – and avoid aggravating local economic inequities by transplanting techniques and methods that aid the wealthy by taking jobs from the poor before means of replacing them are available.

4

Increase opportunities for Latin American students to go to the United States for training. Whether such students come for a six-weeks short course, for a year of special college study, or for a university degree, each is a potential propagandist who according to his state of mind on going home can inoculate a community with rancor or with good will. There should be many more of these visiting students; but only if we determine to do a better job of selecting them and of supervising the treatment they get while here.

It is almost useless to set up fellowships and scholarships if they are to be turned over to local governments for distribution. Most of them go to relatives of officials, and this not only fails to get the best material up here but spreads bitterness among the people there. I recently heard a young Central American say in a public meeting, or rather, shout in a public meeting, that our State Department specializes in awarding fellowships to the sons of government officials. The accusation, which was voiced with considerable feeling, received the almost unanimous applause of the other Latin Americans present. Whether or not it was just, it means that we should lean over backward in an attempt to allocate scholarship funds on a basis of merit alone and to keep them out of the hands of politicians.

The propaganda value of seeding among Caribbean communities students who return pleased with what they saw and learned here can hardly be overestimated, and it seems evident that the full possibilities of this contact are not being fully exploited. Time and again visiting students are dumped into regular academic curricula without proper orientation, to flounder for a year and waste valuable time. Even when academic counseling is adequate there may be little or no attempt to help them get the most out of their extracurricular time.

Donors of scholarship funds will realize on their investment only when they begin to examine more critically the regimen and experiences in store for their charges. Too often visiting students spend their class time studying agricultural techniques applicable chiefly to our own Midwest or pore over texts in sanitary engineering that might more economically have been sent to them at home. The lad selected to be his tropical country's first wildlife technician studies game management in a beech-maple forest or fisheries methods in a Michigan trout stream.

Unless we recognize too that the average Latin American student is a sensitive individual, and make up our minds to baby him a little, we might better leave him at

41

home. He is in strange surroundings here and requires special attention to keep him happy. He must be sheltered from the kind of people who show him how to flush a toilet or ask him who Simón Bolívar was. After I had lived among Latins for a couple of years, I wasn't particularly astonished when one of them admitted to me that his dislike of gringos as a breed dated from the day a professor at a university in the southern United States asked him if he had ever tasted ice cream before coming to this country.

The four-year candidate for a degree may have time to work out his destiny, but the special one-year man and the short course student are at our mercy. And if they have a shoddy time of it — either in class or out — we lose doubly, since our dollars buy not good will but dislike.

5

Support the expansion of public health program. Initiate research into the biology of important parasites not now receiving attention and devise means of applying current findings to extend clinical aid, perhaps on the "county nurse level," to the many rural areas in which amebiasis, malaria, and hookworm combine with the exhaustion of the land to make a squalor of existence that would be hard to duplicate elsewhere in the world.

6

Accelerate and expand agricultural research and education. Set up more experiment stations and distribute them in such a way as to build a stable foundation for animal husbandry, horticulture, and agronomy in all the

diverse environments of the American tropics. As in the
case of public health, a major problem is the lag that always precedes the general application of advanced methods and that should be attacked by scattering agricultural
schools about the countryside. A dozen schools like Escuela Agrícola Panamericana would not be too many, but
we should keep them simple and practical — dedicated to
the training of farmers and possibly of the county agent
type of demonstration worker but not of research men or
engineers, or of office staff for the ministries.

7

Encourage and help the Latin American countries in
establishing and maintaining campaigns of conservation
and restoration of renewable resources.

Of the three principal areas in which technical help
from us is most badly needed — nutrition, public health,
and conservation — the last seems to me at once the most
basic and the field in which the least is being done. It is
surely the most difficult.

When William Vogt published his *Road to Survival,* a
great many people saw in it just a revival of the old
jeremiads of Thomas Malthus and pointed to the details
in which Malthus turned out to be wrong to show that
Vogt too was wrong. They thought Vogt was excitable
and his generalizations too broad, and they accused him
of trying to scare people.

They were right, of course. He was trying to scare
people. Whether his tactics were good or bad I won't try
to say, but I used to get scared before I ever read Vogt.
Whether or not you approve of Vogt or know anything

43

about world demography, you can't ignore the tragic dependence of the peons of Latin America on ruined or wasting environments.

I know a man who is in charge of a heavily subsidized enterprise on a tropical island. The island was once a pleasant place with woods and soil; it now has only scrub and rocks and a population in which poverty and disease are rife and the infant mortality rate appalling. When he was asked if it wasn't time for his wealthy backers to establish a clinic on the island my friend said, "We can't do it. We'd wreck the place completely. It won't hold any more people. It won't hold what it's got. The land's no good and the water's too deep for poor men to fish in."

"But it's inhuman not to save lives when it would be so easy," it was suggested. "The increase could go somewhere else where life would be feasible."

"The increase couldn't go anywhere," said my friend. "It would stay right here and starve with the rest. If you want to save lives go somewhere else to do it."

In this case the problem is diagrammatically clear because the setting is a little island. Perhaps my friend's solution was too simple. Certainly it was shocking; but whether you regard it as manslaughter or as altruism is not just now so important as that you see clearly that such things really happen.

One Sunday afternoon my wife and I were riding back from *Doña* Rosa's llano by way of the Yeguare River trail in the mountains of Honduras. When we came to the ford we stopped and sat on a rock while the hot horses drank. From downstream we heard a report like that of half a stick of dynamite in deep water.

"That's where the fish go," I growled.

There came another clap, closer than the first and sharper, and Margie said, "It doesn't sound like dynamite to me. It sounds like somebody cracking rocks."

We sneaked along the wooded shore, rounded a bend, and saw two men on a bar across the river. As we watched, one of them picked up a big rock, raised it high above his head, and banged it down upon another boulder that lay half submerged in the shallows. Immediately both men crouched and heaved at the implanted stone, turned it over, and started snatching at things in the water around it, pausing now and then to stow away under the crowns of their hats something too small for us to see. They were obviously fishing. They were using the paralyzing concussion of one rock falling on another of equal weight to stun whatever little cavernicolous creatures might be hiding underneath, and we later learned that these were tiny cichlid fishes, and wormlike eels, tadpoles, inch-long frogs, and bug-small crabs and shrimps.

By and by the men stopped fishing and made a fire on the bar, kindling it with splinters of fat ocote pine from a net bag that one carried, and stoking it with driftwood. They put the handful of animals they had caught into a clay cup and propped this on stones to boil over the fire, meanwhile taking from the bag a few limp tortillas rolled in a gray rag.

Before we grew impatient the cooking was finished and the men began taking the little scalded animals from the pot and rolling them in *tortillas* to make crude tamales which they ate with relish. When the meal was over they rose and splashed upstream to another bar, and by the time we had walked back to our horses the banging had begun again, and another installment of the pitiful clambake was under way.

As time passed we grew accustomed to the booming of the rock-bar gleaners, but we never got inured to its implications. Why did the *pencos* have to scrabble for bugs among the rocks? Why did the river give so little to the people who needed so much? Was it wholly because of an occasional stick of dynamite filched from the silver mine and dropped into a river hole? Would a simple program of wardenship make a productive stream of the Yeguare and of a hundred others like it?

The answer was not so easy. It lay rather in the bare bedrock and raw ash under the hillside pines where, since forgotten times, the April fires have run loose, and on the clean-cut mountain tops where the rains of June skim the good from the old soil and dump it into flash-flooded barrancas.

Overnight the quiet river becomes a storm sewer, and the brown tons of water that rip down its bed disrupt and sweep away or suffocate with silt every living thing except a few timid creatures small and shrewd enough to spend their time under stones.

Every biologist who stays long in the tropics is eventually asked about fish culture or urged to make recommendations for restocking some body of water with fish. The people are beginning to hear of our farm ponds in the United States and of our fish planting and to see in restocking a cure-all for any case of unproductivity in their own streams, just as they snatch at such direct and yet technical-sounding devices as artificial insemination as the solution to all their problems of beef and milk production.

But in this country our fish technicians learned a long time ago that restocking is a makeshift that hardly ever cures a stream of unproductivity. Fish depletion is not to be handled as a problem apart but as a symptom of a more general and basic disorder. The river is lean because the land is lean, and the ills of the two cannot be treated separately. Forests, wildlife, and hydraulic heads are all parts of an integrated whole, and none suffers or is restored separately. The river is sterile because the hillside above it is sterile. The firewood famine in the city and the diminishing water supply are not separate afflictions but different signs of the same disaster. Fishing is poor in the high tropics for the same reasons that a thousand miles of night driving on the highways shines no eyes of wild things.

The idea that tropical America is still an unspoiled wilderness dies hard. The average North American is surprised to learn that the Latin countries have any depletion problems at all, and is frankly incredulous when told of their urgency. Moreover, despite scattered stirrings of a realization of the situation, there is a puzzling lethargy among organizations concerned with inter-American good will to appreciate the bearing of landscape restoration on social stability and thus on our own relations with our neighbors. Helping them start saving and rebuilding their lands is more than just good propaganda. It strikes at the heart of the economic plight of the peon and of the basic cause of our growing insecurity in Pan-America.

A workable plan for restoration and maintenance of a landscape is not easy to devise. The factors involved are complex and their interrelationships almost endless. An immense amount of data on the physical and biological make-up of the region must be gathered before anything that the public can see can be done. Meanwhile, the public has become impatient, and the politicians have turned their support to short-term, quick-yielding schemes. They all must be wooed and cajoled again and the attack on the sickness of the land interrupted while some local symptom is treated with makeshift means. But the intricacy of the problems is no excuse for our ignoring them and their urgency and the huge rewards we might earn by helping in their solution.

It is time we stopped courting Latin American bureaucrats and started courting the people. The people are still in the majority, and it is their favor that we need if we are to stay in and Communism to stay out. It is the people who are showing the unrest — not the politicians and diplomats. We must search out every means of bypassing the conventional channels of inter-Americanism, and wherever possible deal directly with the people who are doing the suffering, out in the places where the suffering is being done. The ministers are not suffering; they don't need our help.

The politicians will get along all right. And while we dicker with them the little Indian on the scorched hillside will walk three miles to plant his milpa and seven to till his beans, and his wife will spend half of every day toiling up the rock trail with the day's water from a *vega* mudhole.

It is this little Indian who is growing restless, in one Indo-American nation after another, and it is his good will we may someday want badly. The old way was to keep him ignorant, but that won't work much longer. Time after time his restlessness has surmounted ignorance and degradation and has organized and gained some trifling advantage, and each time we have lost because we were not party to his struggle but more often aided the forces that sought to keep him down. There is no way to keep the peon from learning that there are less brutish ways to live; and there is no way to avert the disaster of his learning except to help him.

From this wry and starkly opportunistic point of view no aspect of our relations with the Caribbean countries seems more important than helping them salvage their landscapes. No agency for hemispheric solidarity and no foreign industrial operation in the tropics can afford to ignore the rewards that await sound, sincere programs of research in the natural science of renewable resource conservation in the wasting lands around the Caribbean.

PART TWO

People in the Land

Sketches of the Hill People

BRIOSA LA YEGUA

THE *canícula* was ending. Big clouds rolled up out of the Mosquitia and there was rain in all the high ranges across the frontier in Nicaragua.

I goaded the old Ford pickup down the road from Jamastran to Danlí. If we lost the race with the rain we would get through only with the help of oxen or a tractor, and we had duties back at school the next day.

As we jolted down the side of a ravine between steep clay banks that rose within two feet of either side of the car, a man approached on horseback from the opposite direction. On the saddle before him he held a baby girl perhaps seven months old. The horse was a gray mare, a pacer, and we remarked on the lively clip at which it came on. The man was dressed in his best, obviously for an occasion.

When the mare reached a point thirty feet in front of the car, she began to prance and weave and balk. I im-

53

mediately stopped the car. The rider spurred the horse but she refused to advance. She reared suddenly and the baby was thrown through the air in a wide arc to land squarely on its back in the trembling mud, where it lay embedded, smiling.

The hysteria of the horse mounted. It bucked and plunged back and forth over the supine baby. The man tried to dismount but lost his balance, and his foot hung in the stirrup. Chable and I jumped from opposite sides of the car, in our haste abandoning it to gravity. I seized the baby by one leg and tried to grab the bridle of the horse; but I missed the hold. The car was moving toward us, unguided and gathering momentum on the muddy incline. Chable vaulted back into the seat in time to keep the car from pinning the horse and dangling rider against the wall.

Suddenly the man's foot slipped from the stirrup. He fell, then picked himself up from the mud and rose, beating his bedraggled garments with his hands. He glanced briefly at the child which I was holding. His gaze moved to the panting mare and rested there. A smile cracked the mud on his face.

¿Briosa la yegua, verdad? he beamed. "Spirited the mare, no?"

Pig Train

THE patience and endurance of the poor mountain people are displayed in the amazing journeys which they make on foot. The sheer doggedness exhibited on these trips always moves me peculiarly to a point between pity and anger. Whole barefoot families, including children of four or five years and even infants in arms, will strike out through rain and mud or merciless sun to walk halfway across the republic. A man on the opposite side of the mountain from the school gets up at three o'clock in the morning and hoists to his shoulder a yoke from which twenty-five braided grass rings hang horizontally. In each ring their rests a two- or three-pound chicken. The man walks fifteen miles with this load, crossing a 6,000-foot range of mountains to reach his destination. If he sells the chickens he returns to his home the same day. Two or three times a week an old woman comes to the cross-roads above the school to sell fruit. She walks eight miles down a rocky trail and in that distance descends two thousand feet from her home on the mountain. She carries thirty pounds of quinces or mangoes in a broad basket on her head. She too goes home the same day.

One night as I was driving along a country road I noticed flickering firelight some distance ahead. As I approached, I saw that the light was cast by a torch of fat pine held high by a man who moved almost imperceptibly down the center of the road. He was an unusually tall and very gaunt and ragged figure. He wore one of the high, conically-crowned hats common in the El Paraíso district. He plodded in the dust with his face straight forward and with the fixed introversion of a somnambulist. As I drew up alongside I saw that he was driving pigs. From his belt there hung a bag of pebbles, and every few steps he took a pebble from the bag and tossed it mechanically at the hindmost pig.

I stopped the car and looked at the pigs. The man gave me a brief glance but the pigs paid no notice whatever.

They shuffled painfully along in a tight little band of nine, just in front of the man. They all wore rawhide shoes. They were half-grown shoats that had weighed perhaps ninety pounds when they left home. They now weighed about sixty pounds. Dressed, at market, they would bring fifty centavos, which is twenty-five cents gold, a pound.

I contemplated the half-live man and his torch and the weary pigs and their silly-looking shoes, and was moved to ask, "Where have you come from?" "From Jamastran," he said, without interest. "Going to Tegucigalpa?" I asked. "Yes," he said. *Adiós.*

Tegucigalpa lay seventeen miles beyond and Jamastran fifty-two miles behind.

Adiós, I said as he moved on. I turned the key in the ignition switch and sat in silence, watching the receding light of the pine torch.

The Saint and the Zebras

WE climbed the rocky path leading up to the little mud house with the sagging tile roof. It was obvious that the occupants were aware of our approach, for through the open door we could see the old woman beating wildly at the floor with a cornshuck broom. There was another woman whom we did not know. She was young and in the last stages of pregnancy and had on a shapeless black garment which her distended abdomen stretched to the point of bursting. As we approached the door we saw that she was trying to disengage a dirty piece of bed ticking that was tangled about the neck and shoulders of an emaciated child. The child was incredibly filthy and its gray-ish hair stood out from its head like an old rope end. Its nose ran, the glands in its neck were swollen, and its face was the color of dough under the dirt.

The old woman made a few ineffectual last strokes at the floor, threw the broom behind her into the darkness of the kitchen, and turned to greet us.

Pasen adelante, she croaked.

Old age and poverty are not frequently seen together in Honduras, but this shrivelled, toothless woman was old by any standards. She was a relic of the days when silver could be scratched from the mountain. The little community was busy and prosperous then, and many a mule scrambled up Cerro Grande bound for Tegucigalpa with two shining ingots on its back. She patted my wife's shoulders, and her words of greeting had a strange, pleasant quality compounded of Indian ceremony and the elegance of dead Spaniards and the sentimentality of her own great age. She turned toward the girl who was still trying to remove the wrappings from the sick child. *Vení, Maruja,* she said. "Here is the lady who visited me the other time."

As our eyes became adjusted to the gloom of the windowless interior, we dimly made out the figures of three more sexless children against the far wall. Each wore a single sack-like garment that had originally been black but that now was of the same curious gray color as the skin and hair of its wearer. The three stood and scratched themselves almost rhythmically and stared at us with bright eyes.

From under a rickety bed there staggered a half-feathered chicken. Its head was sunk between its wings.

Its rump and legs were plastered with feces and bits of trash. As it tried to walk its boneless legs bent and twisted and it flopped across the floor in a revolting series of spasmic jerks. The pregnant girl kicked it toward the bed, where it fell and lay in convulsions.

My wife made a gesture toward a leaning table on which there was a little shrine with a plaster saint. Before the shrine stood several pots and jars of flowers, some of them artificial and some recently gathered from the field. The saint had a silver halo, and on either side of the shrine stood two china zebras. The incongruity of the shrine in its setting was so striking that it did not occur to me to wonder where the Victorian zebras had come from or why in the world my wife wanted them.

Ah, sí, los animalitos, rasped the old woman. "They are pretty."

"And have you decided to sell them to me? You said before that you would consider the matter."

The old woman looked at the zebras and rubbed her gums together while she meditated on the strength of her temptation. At length she reached a decision, and the set depth of the wrinkles of her face showed that it was a final one.

Qué lástima, Señora, she said. "It is a pity, because we are poor and need the money, but the *animalitos* cannot be sold. They are not mine to sell. They are of the saint."

The Nursing Viper

OUR barber at the school is a small, rather intelligent man by the name of Velásquez. Purely by coincidence he, too, paints pictures, and his work has been seen and called primitive modern by several erudite visitors — whether in disparagement or in praise I am not prepared to say.

Velásquez has a cleft palate and his Spanish is hard to understand, but what he says is frequently very sound or very colorful and is often worth sweating over. I have learned a great many things from him.

Not long ago I stopped by the tiny room where Velásquez holds forth, to get a haircut. I was carrying a quart fruit jar which contained a small, poisonous snake of the genus *Bothrops*. I placed the jar on the floor and sat down in the barber chair. Velásquez walked over to the jar, looked in, and turned away. "Terrible animal," he muttered as he picked up his comb and scissors.

Among Velásquez' talents is a fine, if somewhat disapproving, feeling for natural history. I settled myself in the chair and prepared to learn something extraordinary.

"What's so bad about the snake?" I asked. "It looks to me as if it's too small to be very dangerous." This was exactly what the barber wanted.

"It's little, all right, but in my estimation it is the worst of all the snakes we have. It is called *casera* because it enters houses. Because of its small size it can get into any house, crawling through cracks or under the door. But it lives mostly in houses of nursing mothers."

This was enough to quicken anyone's interest and it did mine, but I didn't interrupt. He went on.

"The *casera* comes out of the cracks during the night. It climbs the bedpost and gets under the bedclothes with the nursing woman and noses about until it finds her bosom. Then it takes a nipple in its mouth."

I could not restrain myself. "And bites," I suggested.

"No, sucks," said Velásquez. "It nurses. It likes mother's milk better than anything else. Sometimes it just nurses and then crawls away. This is disgusting but not tragic. The really bad part comes if the baby awakes hungry while the snake is there. If the child seeks comfort at the occupied breast, the viper coils at once into a tight ball. The doomed infant, fumbling for the nipple, takes instead the coiled snake into its mouth. Thereupon the *casera* shows its true character. It crawls down into the child's stomach and strikes repeatedly at all vitals within reach. The infant shrieks, but it is too late for help."

"Does it swell up and turn black and die?" I ventured.

"Why, yes." Velásquez was surprised and a little hurt with me for anticipating him. I looked down at the jar on the floor. Through the glass I could see the bright, unblinking eyes of the monstrous little viper.

"It's the worst snake we have," said the barber.

The Contrabandist

THE lonely windblown *rancho* stood back of the beach, a dozen feet from the drifted wrack of springtide reach, and half hidden among the sea oats. We beached our dugout and walked toward the little shack, the mushy, gray pumice-sand rising between our bare toes at each step.

"Let me do the talking," said Titeo. That was all right with me. I knew that Titeo was as able at persuasion as he was at fishing. He spoke the ungrammatical staccato Spanish of the Fonseca native with glib, aggressive drive that nearly always got him what he wanted. He was an odd character all around. He had Indian features and a mop of curly hair and a black skin. He was a cheerful gamin of a man with no shoes and no respect for anybody. He was the only Honduranean I ever met who used the *vos*-form of address with me — a gringo — from the the outset of our acquaintance. He had no money and no inhibitions and he didn't give a damn. I had engaged him to help me in my campaign to learn something about the sea turtles of the Gulf of Fonseca and he was a good choice.

"The *dueño* of this *rancho* is a *contrabandista.* His name's Orozco," said Titeo.

"What do you mean? What does he smuggle, and where?" I looked about the desolate landscape behind the island beach, over the low scrub of buttonwood and manchineel to the waste of red mangrove swamp laced by the estuaries that separated us from the mainland.

"Himself," said Titeo. "He's not a Honduranean, he's from that island over there," and he motioned to a low rise of land seaward of the symmetrical cone of Tigre Island. "His island's in El Salvador and the beach doesn't serve. The turtles don't put their eggs there except for a few *careyes*, and Orozco paddles over here in his *cayuca* and stays three months out of the year and digs eggs. And this is Honduras." Titeo felt he should be indignant.

"What does he do with the eggs besides eat them?" I said.

"When he gets a *cayuca* full he paddles over to La Union and sells them. He gets more than they pay for hen's eggs."

"What does he do the rest of the year when the turtles aren't laying?" I asked.

"Nothing. He fishes a little, I guess. But mostly he just waits for the turtles to start laying again. They start coming on the beach in August and keep coming till November. He makes enough then to last the rest of the year. He doesn't need much."

I was ready to accept this, since we now had a good view of the Orozco residence.

Orozco was sitting on an upturned dugout in front of his shack. He was a slim, small man with a mournful face and a pendent, stringlike moustache. He wore a ragged pair of canvas pants, and for a shirt a long, buttonless garment that hung to his knees like an old-fashioned nightgown. He was smoking a frayed cigar, hand-rolled from the small black tobacco leaves that you can grow in the back yard. We must have been the first visitors he'd had that week, if not that month, but he didn't look at us. Instead, he gazed steadily out over the Gulf, past the islands of Honduras, toward the Pacific horizon and the dim volcanoes of his native land.

"I've just been sitting here watching the sunset," he said. "You know, you can sit right here like I'm sitting now and see three countries without moving your head. See, watch."

We looked at him and sure enough, his head was still as a rock and his eyes were rolling rhythmically back and forth through the majestic panorama that spread before us: right, center, left, center, right; from the tall island volcanoes of Tigre and Zacate Grande on the Honduranean side through a deep spread of near and far islands of El Salvador, with the perfect cone of San Miguel smoking gently in the blue distance of the mainland; and on around through an arc of open sea to the fractured body of Coseçüina, the Nicaraguan volcano that made "the year of the great darkness" when it exploded in 1838 with the loudest noise men had yet known. When his eyes got tired Orozco stopped and rose and shook hands limply, first with Titeo, then with me.

Titeo stood up straight and began to function in his capacity of intermediary.

"This man is a scientific," he said. "He wants to watch the turtles lay tonight. He doesn't want the eggs and he doesn't molest turtles. He wants to see what they do. The *coronel* at the coast guard office says for you *hueveros,* especially the contraband ones, to stay off the beach till the *señor* goes away."

"All right," said Orozco. "It is a thing that can. Let's go inside. The *jejenes* are starting to bite."

We followed him into the *rancho.* It offered little protection against anything, and none at all against the blood-mad little sandflies we had come in to escape. It was four poles and a high-peaked roof of palm thatch. There were no walls except on the two sides where the roof came nearly to the ground. A network hammock hung diagonally across the interior. In back three stones made a fireplace on the sand floor. On these sat Orozco's kitchenware: a clay pot, a tin can for making coffee, and a clay dish that doubled as a frying pan. At one side a big water gourd stood, with a corncob stopper on which there hung a *jicaro* cup.

At least half the floor area, including all that under the hammock, was smoothly paved with a layer of turtle eggs half embedded in the sand and so closely spaced that they looked like curious hemispherical tiles on a bathroom floor. Titeo noticed my astonishment and said, "Turtle eggs last a long time that way."

Sientense, said Orozco. "In the hammock. I'll get you some salt and you can eat some eggs while we talk." He brought a clam shell full of gray salt, set a chile pod on the edge, and put the shell among the eggs under the hammock, at the same time handing each of us half a lemon.

"Eat all you want," he said.

We began eating turtle eggs. Orozco sat and watched us. I thought what a mess it would be if he ever got restless at night and fell out of the hammock with the mosaic of eggs underneath.

Titeo was sucking eggs twice as fast as I was. *Savrosas,* he said. All his indignation was gone. "We hardly ever get any in San Lorenzo these days. I'm going to take a bag back to my *compañera.* She always likes me better when she eats a lot of turtle eggs."

"Are you still living with that Marta from Amapala?" said Orozco.

"No. Girl named Juana Rivas. She came from San Miguel, I think. She's all right but she's pretty wild."

"There you are, see," said Orozco, speaking with more spirit than he had shown before. "They're all wild nowadays. None of them seem to know how to act around a house, at least not any I can find. That's why I live alone. In some ways it convenes to have a woman around, but I don't know — ." His eyes moved about the dwelling and stopped on a small, black, dried fish that hung by a reed from a rafter. *Cuesta formalizarlas,* he said. "It's just too hard to train them up. It disheartens a man, at least it does me, to go to all the trouble of finding a girl he wants to live with and to bring her into his home and then find she doesn't know how to act and doesn't want to learn."

He pushed the last half-inch of his unravelling cigar into the sand bottom of a little pit where an egg had been, sighed, and looked out at the red globe the sun had become as it dipped toward the far islands.

"You're right," said Titeo. "That's just the way it goes."

He reached for another turtle egg, pinched a hole in it, gave it a quick squeeze of lemon and noisily sucked it out of the leathery shell; and then he lay back in the hammock with his head on his hands, and his gaze followed Orozco's out over the dancing red waves of the Gulf toward the darkening Pacific.

Mules and Horseplay

The Coming of the Bulls

IT was nine o'clock in the evening and the Subdirector was irritable. For one thing, he had threatened to fire Midence that morning. Midence was *mayordomo* of the school ranch and nobody liked to cross him. Not that he didn't usually deserve it, for he was nearly always full of *guaro*, at times dangerously so. But he always carried a pistol and claimed to have used it to kill men, and no one doubted his word. He had a good farm at the end of the valley and nobody knew exactly why he wanted to work for the school. The school didn't really need his services either, but it wanted his good will, as long as it didn't come too high. Midence had been reprimanded for getting drunk before and had surprised everyone by taking it meekly enough. But the Subdirector hadn't enjoyed it that time or this.

Besides that, he had waited around all afternoon fretting while we crawled up the hundred miles of rocky road with the two Guernsey bulls we were hauling up from the coast in a borrowed truck. And now the loading ramp had been misplaced, and we couldn't find it in the dark.

We stood around jawing at each other for a while, making one impracticable proposal after another for getting the bulls out of the truck without a ramp. The Sub-director's wife, Margaret, and my wife, Margie, stood nearby, and offered a few suggestions which we ignored on principle. Finally it occurred to us to go up the road a way where there was an embankment of about the same height as the platform of the truck. It ought to be a simple matter to back the truck up to the bank and just lead the bulls off and onto the ground.

As the driver was maneuvering the truck into position crosswise in the road and everybody was shouting directions back and forth, a form loomed in the darkness. It was Midence riding his mule. Midence's mule was a small, compact buckskin with tiny feet and a tight hide. It was the best mountain mule in the valley and Midence was proud of it. He had refused two hundred lempiras for it, and had trimmed its tail in fancy terraces and always used a scrolled Spanish bit and a martingale and an elegant crupper with white pom-poms. Behind him, on the mule's rump, clinging precariously to Midence's back, rode a lean and ancient man with a long, wire-stiff chin-beard. Both were very drunk on *guaro*, the abrasive, demoralizing government rum.

When Midence saw the truck moving backward across the road and the bulls in it, the *mayordomo* in him was stimulated to take charge. He shouted and waved his hat and spurred the mule toward the rapidly narrowing space between the truck and the bank. The Subdirector yelled and tried to turn the mule, but the trio lurched past him to what seemed sure destruction. They dashed into the gap, now only three feet wide. The women screamed together, and the real dread in their cries must have got through to Midence somehow. He suddenly saw his predicament, spurred the now frantic mule with overdue desperation, and shot from the closing gap with one knee touching the truck and the other scraping clay from the bank. He shouted again, presumably in triumph. He reined up the mule, turned it, sprang at the embankment, and tried to goad the hysterical animal into climbing the nearly vertical face. The mule reared and clawed at the clay. The old man slid off and fell to the ground. He landed solidly on a bottle of *guaro* in his hip pocket and demolished it. The women shrieked again, softly this time, and the aroma of *guaro* drifted about.

Relieved of their incubus, Midence and the mule scrambled to the top of the bank, where Midence stopped and reached down, seized the hand of the dejected Subdirector, and shook it happily.

The old man with the beard rose slowly from the ground. He looked about until his blurred gaze fell on Margaret and Margie standing on the far road shoulder. He walked toward the cowering women, picking broken glass from his pocket and dropping it to the ground.

¡Ay, qué muchachonas! he roared. "What are you girls doing the rest of the evening?"

The driver peered from the cab of the truck, craning his neck to see what was going on.

¡Qué relajo! he muttered. "What a disorder!"
The Subdirector's day was complete.

THE FORD

Holy Week — 1945

THE goggle diver rose from the sparkling depths of the pool beside the ford. His sudden appearance in the golden sunshine above the crystal surface was startling and outrageously incongruous. The cold water had turned his thin body a curious shade of blue, an impure shade, like neither the aquamarine of the pool nor the turquoise of the sky. He trembled convulsively and tried to gulp air and expel water at one time from his wide-open mouth. The upper part of his face and head were incased in a section of automobile inner tube closed in front by a six-inch pane of glass. His hands clawed for a hold on the slick wet rocks. He combined the less pleasant features of a Cyclops and a Caliban in a setting not used to such horror. It is doubtful if any Honduranean river ever saw the like. Certainly it was something new at the Morocelí ford.

For some time the thin, blue diver sat shivering and gasping on a half-sunk boulder. Then he raised his hands to his mask and fumbled at it through his racking ague. He lifted it from his face to blow his nose, and up the trail he saw the van of a mule train descending to the ford from the rocky cliff above. The foremost mule bore a large woman who sat her side saddle with patience and dignity. The animal emerged from the low brush of the river bank and clattered over the rocks toward the edge

of the water. The diver, unseen by either the mules or
the people of the train, adjusted his mask, slid from the
rock, and sank to the bottom of the pool. He lay there
and tried to smile devilishly and the result was awful.

As his mule picked her way delicately down the rocky
slope toward the ford, Adán Callejas was happy. The day
was fine and half the trip from Tabla Grande to Morocelí
lay behind. His mules bore his entire family and four
cargas of quinces besides, which he would sell at profit in
Morocelí. He would spend Holy Week in idleness and
revelry. He looked with affection toward his wife Manuela, who was five mules ahead, approaching the ford.

As Manuela Callejas' mule stopped fetlock deep and
noisily sucked the clear cold water, the impossible occurred. From the pool twelve feet away there slowly
emerged a head with one gigantic eye. The eye was open
wide and was fixed upon Manuela. With horrible delibera-
tion a skinny bluish torso came up under the head. Manuela tried to call the others. She could make no sound but
only thrashed wildly with her arms. The creature in the
pool gazed steadily at the woman and exhaled suddenly
from somewhere, causing the black flaps on its cheeks to vi-
brate with an intolerable blatting sound. The mule reared
and wheeled and scrambled back across the cobbled shore,
while the woman shouted hoarsely. Somehow the two
stayed together, but they collided with the first pack
mule and threw the train into confusion.

The diver repented his abortive horseplay. He floundered to the shore, rose, and ran toward the chattering
people, tearing at his mask. He stood before them in re-

pulsive humility. "I'm sorry," he said, "It was a joke. I hope you're not hurt."

The Callejas stared at him. A little girl whimpered. Manuela lost all vestige of control. *¡Ay dios, ay mi madre, ay mi madre!* she wailed. Adán started whipping the mules. He herded them all into the water, and kept whipping them all the way across the river till they climbed the opposite bank into the trail to Morocelí.

¿Qué fué, Mama? the little girl keened. *Ay, mi madre,* moaned Manuela, as the train disappeared around the bend in the trail.

Holy Week — 1946

¡Carajo! said Cruz in great disgust as the big thunderhead slid down the mountainside and large drops of rain began to spatter on the rocks. The blue pool by the ford grew gray and opaque as the raindrops punched deep little holes and sent concentric rings of disturbance scurrying and colliding across the surface. Prospects for goggling in beautiful Río Cobre were dim. Chable and Cruz had long ago planned this trip on which Jeanie was to be initiated into the blessed group of humans who have goggled in Cobre in the sunshine. They had come far and now there would be no goggling and they would get wet anyway. As the cold drops fell faster, melancholy settled over the trio in spite of their youth.

They stood beneath the feather-leaved *guanacaste* tree beside the ford and shivered at the outlook. Chable walked over to the horses and untied from his saddle a rolled United States Army raincoat. From Jeanie's saddle he took a green plastic slicker with a hood. Cruz had no raincoat. "Do you mind sitting on my shoulders?" he asked Jeanie. "I suppose not," said Jeanie, who was docile by nature and used to Cruz's caprice. She walked over to where Cruz was kneeling on the ground and sat on the back of his neck. He rose with her. Chable put the big raincoat around Jeanie's shoulders and it fell to Cruz' waist. Chable then put on Jeanie's shiny plastic slicker and pulled the hood over his head, leaving only his big sunburnt nose sticking out. The little group stood against the trunk of the tree and waited. The rain fell harder.

¡Carajo! said Adán Callejas as rain began to fall on his mule train. "Yes, it is going to rain, but hard," said his wife Manuela, "and already has a cold Mechitas." "Well, we can't stop now," said Adán irritably. "If we stop on this side of the river and it rises we will have to go back home." None of the family wanted to go back home and miss Holy Week in Morocelí.

As the lead mule, which carried Manuela Callejas, passed the big *guanacaste* tree by the ford, it shied viciously and jumped from the bank into the water. Only her powerful reflexive grip on the long curved horn of the sidesaddle saved Manuela from falling. As her mount dashed into the water and ploughed across the river, Manuela looked back over her shoulder toward the tree and saw the nine-foot blonde girl with dripping hair and her weird hooded companion.

¡Ay, dios! shrieked Manuela, *¡ay mi madre!* Adán began running his horse back and forth behind the train, flailing the hindmost mules. *Otra vez,* he muttered bitterly, unaware of what was wrong but sure heaven was against him. As each animal passed the tree, it shied, laid

back its ears, and jumped forward into the water. As his own mule entered the stream Adán looked back. He saw the people under the tree. He flinched a little, and then spurred and whipped his mule so that it plunged across the river and up the other bank, where it joined the others trotting off rapidly down the trail. The children were quiet but Manuela was still moaning, *Ay, mi madre.*

"The next time," said Adán, "we should take the upper ford."

Olancho Backwater

THE first time I saw Olancho I went no farther than the eastern side of the mountains beyond Guaimaca, but even this glimpse was enough to show that here was something different. We rounded a bend beyond Las Flores and abruptly got the trade wind in our eyes, and there was a different feel to the air and face to the forest. We stayed long enough to watch a cloud move up out of the ravine heads below and whip itself to shreds among the liquidambar trees; and then another cloud shut out the view and we turned to go back over the ridge. As we moved away there was a distant shout and clink of metal, and we looked out through a hole in the mist and saw the figures of two men in the yard of a little shack on a far hillside. They were slashing at each other with machetes and even the distance did not dull the high fury of their movements. Other people — men, women, and children — were running out of the house and fragments of their yells

74

drifted over to our side of the valley. Then the mist blotted them all out, and for two minutes we had only tag ends of angry sound from across the valley to keep us in touch with the drama. When the cloud thinned out again, one of the cutlassmen was lying on the ground with ropes wound around his body and two men standing over him, while the other was stalking about the clearing waving his arms and shouting curses too far to hear but not to understand.

This was my introduction to Olancho. I mention the incident, because it and the virgin trade wind and the change in the forest seemed to show that the people who have always said Olancho was a land apart, where anything could happen, were right.

The people of the rest of Honduras have an odd and unsettled attitude toward the Department of Olancho. They are proud that this vast, romantic land with its fat, flat plains and golden sands lies on their side of Río Coco and not across it in Nicaragua; but at the same time they stand in some awe of the place with its remote towns and independent people, and disapprove of the wild, meaningless place names that have drifted up the Patuca from the Mosquitia. It is a land of diversity and great contrasts, a frontier four centuries and a quarter old, with the blood of the first wave of conquistadores in its people and men still wild along its lowland streams. It has given the republic a lot of trouble and some of its most illustrious citizens as well. Opinions of Olancho diverge because some people like color in a state, while others like roads and predictable politics. Hardly anybody goes there, but everyone is conscious of the place and the aura of mystery and promise about it, and everywhere you hear that it has more future than any other major area of Central America.

The second time I saw Olancho, Al Chable and I went with Mario Valenzuela of Tegucigalpa to bring out a planeload of mahogany from a little sawmill that he had flown out and put together on the Guampu River in the far Olanchan Mosquitia. Hauling lumber by airplane may seem like a queer business, but mahogany had just reached four hundred dollars a thousand in the United States and the scheme seemed good to Mario. It seemed good to Chable and me, too, because otherwise we would never have got to the Guampu River.

We stayed only four hours. Chable and I seined in the Guampu and talked with the first Paya Indians we had ever seen and found a tapir track. When the plane was loaded we climbed in on top of the lumber and took off and almost immediately flew into a squall. It is bad enough to fly through a thunderstorm in a passenger plane with seats and upholstery, but on top of Mario's lumber it was the worst ride I ever had. When a wing dipped we rolled across the planks and banged against the low wall, and when the plane hit an air pocket it dropped out from under us and the lumber, and then caught us up again with a crash that seemed sure to knock the bottom out and that once left me tied up with both hands under the same board I was lying on.

Suddenly we flew out from among the dark thunderheads and the swirling storm towers; and there, spread in the sun, lay the endless plains of Olancho, and directly below us the tiny Indian town with the touching name, Dulce Nombre de Culmi.

Dulce Nombre! Sweet name. Sweet, welcome little cluster of mud *chozas*, beyond the pitching storm, with the old plane settling out straight and level so suddenly she seemed to stop dead in the air; and the boards lying quiet beneath us.

The Spaniards began to speak of the mystery and promise of this land in 1524, when Francisco de Las Casas founded the town of Trujillo where Columbus had first come ashore on the New World mainland. The Spanish nose for gold soon led one party after another into the hinterland to seek the fabulous mines that lay behind the coastal hills. Cortés reached Trujillo, after the most incredible walk the world has ever known, with enough energy left to tame the Indians who molested the new settlement. Word of the new conqueror reached the distant tribes of Olancho, and they sent envoys to declare their submission to the Spanish king and to increase the Spanish pulse rate with gifts of golden *chispas* and quills of dust.

At one time the golden promise of Olancho seemed hardly less than that of Peru and Mexico, but somehow it was never quite fulfilled. Great quantities of gold did come out at first, surely — although no one seems to have even a rough notion of how much — but it was mostly traded or stolen from the Indians, whose women scratched the worn nuggets from dry placers or picked the round grains of the Guayape and the thin flakes of the Jalan from the washings in their cedar bateas. The Spaniards took the gold the Indians brought but the mother lode eluded them, and the mystery of Olancho grew.

The earliest settlement in the interior was San Jorge de

Olancho, founded by Diego de Alvarado in 1530 on the most uncannily ill-fated site he possibly could have found in all the province of Tecultran. But no doubt it seemed a pleasant place, there beside the sleeping Boquerón, with no sign to show that this was the only volcano in Honduras with any fight left in it. The town thrived and soon four thousand Spaniards were there, taking tribute in gold from sixteen thousand Indians and growing fabulously rich; and there are stories still of the golden bits and shoes their horses wore. There is also a story of a golden Virgin built with contributions from the faithful but left standing in the church unfinished when the congregation grew rich and indifferent. For want of gold with which to crown the image the priest made a crown of rawhide, thinking to shame his erring flock, but instead the people sneered at him and snapped their fingers in his face. They got so nasty, in fact, that they brought down upon themselves the wrath of God in the shape of an eruption of Boquerón so terrible that all were killed or driven away and the city destroyed. At least so the tale goes, and certainly there is no San Jorge today, and Boquerón has a big hole in it.

San Jorge was ruined in 1611, and the very next year there was more excitement when Padre Esteban Verdelete and party were killed and eaten by the Payas, who later in the evening got blind drunk drinking beer from the scooped-out skulls of the poor missionaries. A number of them fell off the Patuca bluffs and were killed, and this so sobered the rest that there is no record of a Paya eating anyone since, although I was pleased to hear that some of them still skulk about in the forest with blowguns.

Just to bring this affair up to date: In 1805 Padre Goicoechea founded a town on the Agalta plain and called it San Esteban, in memory of his martyred predecessor; and when I first went to Honduras my friend Father Gabriel, a Franciscan friar in charge of the ancient mission there, used to talk about the quaint and lonesome charm of the place. In spite of the occasional commercial airplane that visits it, San Esteban has apparently changed but little in a hundred years. On one of his rounds on the plain around San Esteban, Father Gabe stopped at the lonely hut of an Indian whose wife was feverish and in great pain from a huge swelling on the side of her abdomen. Unable either to diagnose the case or to do anything to help the poor woman, Father Gabe left some aspirin and rode away with a heavy heart.

Three months later, passing that way again, he stopped at the *choza* expecting to console a widowed *dueño*. Instead, the cheerful voice of the woman greeted him from a cot inside, and the husband took him in to see the healing scar of an incision that the man himself had made with a sheath-knife in his wife's belly wall. For no known reason the woman was clearly getting well.

Even the single-minded Spaniards came to see that the grass of Olancho might prove richer than its gold, and they partly atoned for the demoralizing influence of their gold lust by introducing cattle into the ungrazed plains. Almost at once trains of steers began to crowd the Trujillo trails and these did more than Guayape gold to draw in the *flotas* and *galeones* of the Caribbean.

Cattle made Olancho wealthy and kept it isolated. The good pasturage lay on terrace plains as remote from centers of civilization as any part of Middle America, and the haciendas quickly became self-sufficient. Cattle were driven out to the North Coast, or even to Guatemala and El Salvador, and while mule trains went along to bring back foreign goods the people mostly stayed at home and became quaint and provincial.

They kept clear of the political turmoil that followed the independence of 1821 and had almost no truck with the new central government. They chased recruiting officers and tax collectors back to Comayagua and repelled attacks by federal forces sent to punish them. Encouraged by the British, the King of the Mosquitia came up the Patuca in 1847 to try to annex Juticalpa, and about the same time the English tried unsuccessfully to colonize the lands around the junction of the Guayape and Guayambre rivers. All these people were operating too far from home, and their schemes and connivings worried the Olanchanos hardly at all.

Today a road connects Juticalpa, the chief city of the department, with the capital, but it dies out on the plain beyond Catacamas and has brought little change in the lives of the people. For instance, this is the only place where I ever saw horsemen actually using *cubetas*, the ornate old shoelike brass stirrups that tourists fight for throughout Latin America and that usually must be sought in antique shops. In Olancho you see them on saddles.

I once came upon two *vaqueros* chasing a steer across the dry Lepaguare valley. From the glint of the sun on their stirrups I could see that they were *cubetas*. Both men were swinging rawhide lassos, called here *pialeras*, and as one of them closed with the steer I saw his loop settle over the creature's head. I naturally expected the pony to stop and face the steer to take the shock when the rope ran out; instead, it wheeled and stood with its tail toward the steer, and then I saw that the rope was not dallied about the saddle horn, for there was no saddle horn, but was braided into the doubled hair of the horse's tail. When the steer reached the end of the sixty-foot lasso I winced, fully expecting to see the tail of the pony fly out by the roots, but nothing of the sort happened. When the steer came up short the horse was dragged backward a few feet, but it seemed to feel no pain at all, and the tail held.

The other *vaquero* approached the steer and tossed another loop over its horns; and as the two prepared to drag the animal away, I went over and joined them. I asked them why in the world they tied their lassos to the horses' tails.

They seemed puzzled by the question and their eyes wandered over their horses for a moment. Then one of them looked at me and shrugged.

"There's nothing else to tie them to," he said.

He was right, and I felt embarrassed at the question. I looked at his stirrups.

"Where do you get stirrups like that?" I asked.

Son de antes, said the man. "They are of before."

"But where did they come from? Who made them?" I insisted.

¿Quién sabe, señor? he said, and jerked his arm in a vague gesture toward the past. *Son de antes*.

It seems odd to anybody but an Olanchano that in a city like Juticalpa, which has given Honduras three presidents and even a pair of lady poets, people should still carry their water from the river. There is no municipal water supply in the town; or at least there was none when I was there. Those who can afford it have water delivered by burros, and one morning I accompanied a twelve-year-old *arriero* and his three tank-carrying burros on one of their rounds. The boy was called Chus, which is a nickname for people named Jesus. He drove the three little asses out beyond the fringe of women washing clothes in the shallows of the river, and when they stopped in water up to their bellies he baled the tanks full with a bucket. The tanks were huge affairs of galvanized iron nailed to cedar endpieces, and bent to fit the burros' sides, where they hung like saddle bags. When the tanks were full the boy slapped each burro on the rump to start it up the shore toward the center of town, and he and I followed.

"The middle one is the most intelligent burro in the world," said Chus.

"Really?" I said. "Why do you think that?"

"Just keep looking at him," said Chus.

We entered a narrow street and walked down it a way, past one intersection and into another, and here the middle burro turned to the left, while Chus and the other two kept on straight ahead, paying no mind.

I touched Chus on the shoulder. "We've left the intelligent burro behind," I said. "What's the matter with him? Where's he going?"

Chus beamed with pride. "He's going to deliver his water," he said. "I told you he was smart."

"Wonder if he'd mind if I went along with him," I said.

Claro que no, said Chus. "Nothing bothers him. He's

going to Mrs. Mejia's. She always takes all his water."

I went back to the corner, turned it, and caught up with the burro, following close behind him for a few minutes down a long, straight street where all the houses looked just alike. Suddenly the burro halted beside a pair of closed double doors beside the street. As the clicks of his hooves stopped, a female voice within the house yelled, *¡El agua!* and the doors swung open to show a little beady-eyed doll of a girl child who bolted when she saw me. The burro entered, stepped daintily across the cobbled patio to the open kitchen, and stopped beside a stone water filter. A fat Indian girl started filling the filter from the tanks, and after a bit she noticed me watching from the doorway. She hitched her skirt, and tucked in her breasts.

"What can I offer you?" she called.

"I was just looking at that burro," I said.

Ah, vaya, said the girl, patting the burro on his flat forehead. "This is the most intelligent burro in the world."

The little ass stood with his weight all on three legs, his eyes half closed, and his long ears drooped and jutting sideways. I suppose he was asleep.

"Yes, I know," I said.

The aristocrats of Olancho have not dropped all the old Indian ways, and one pleasant custom that everybody has clung to is the making of coyol wine. To the Mexicans who came down with Cortés there must have been something nostalgically Nahuatlan in the way the Jicaques shinnied up the spiny coyol palms, hollowed out a space in the upper end of the trunk just under the bud, and drew off the bland sap with a reed. The *pulquero* back on the Mexican Plateau didn't have to climb his magueys to tap their honeywater, but otherwise the whole business was much the same, and still is.

Today, in March and April, when the sap has grown strong from the drought, everybody makes *vino de coyol.* They no longer climb the trees, but cut them down instead and haul them home where they can be watched tenderly. Once there, a six-inch cubical chamber is chopped in the bud end of the trunk. This soon fills with sap which in two or three days begins to ferment and makes a delectable live wine not unlike champagne in flavor, although perhaps more like the carbonated hard cider that was sold for champagne in the United States during Prohibition. It is usually drunk through a reed straw straight from the trunk, although some people like to siphon it off and sweeten it with *miel de palo,* the strong, dark honey of tiny stingless bees. As the contents of the tank are used up the walls are shaved with a sharp blade to renew the flow, and this may be done over and over again, till the tree has yielded as much as two or three gallons of wine.

If you have no *coyolal* of your own you can have a trunk delivered to the heart of Juticalpa for two lempiras, or a dollar gold. The experts see important differences in the wines of different trunks, and a family of means may have half-a-dozen sprawled about the patio for appreciative guests to sample and discuss.

Much courting is done head-to-head over two canes in one wine-tank, and a code of manners for elegant coyol drinking has evolved. That is, among the refined townspeople and *hacendados.* Among the Indians the point is still just to get drunk.

Among the many times that Olancho has rebelled against the republic, one of the most serious is said to have been when the people in Tegucigalpa tried to extend the market for *guaro* — the ghastly, government-made cane rum, by taxing *vino de coyol*. The tax was never imposed.

I should like to go back to Olancho, and not for the gold. Too many people have broken their hearts over the gold. It's scattered all to hell and gone, and even most of the Spaniards finally quit trying to find out where it comes from. Let the Indian women and the *gambusinos* scratch together their lemp-a-day in grains of dust and don't begrudge them the rare *chispa* that keeps them scratching.

What I like is the land — the unspoiled, endless land, dropping in sun-washed, tiger-trailed terraces from the cloud forests of the backbone ranges where pineclad ridge follows grassy valley like low waves and troughs of the ocean into the monsoon groves and selvas and palm-pine savannas of Entrerios and the Caribbean shore.

It is an uncluttered land worth living in, where living could be fun again. It is big enough for the most restless, and varied enough for any but the hopeless metrophile. Its climates range from the wheat weather of the high interior to the coconut climate of the Mosquitia, and in between nearly anything worth while can be grown or done.

My last impression of Olancho is oddly in key with the rest. Blas Enriques, Abraham Arce, and I were returning from a steer-buying trip for the school, pounding along the ruinous road from Catacamas to Juticalpa in the brief dusk. Blas, who grew up in Olancho, and still talks like it, was telling us about his boyhood there. In fact he was telling us of the time he rode muleback to the capital during a revolution, and carried in his saddlebag two little party flags, a blue one to wave if he met *azules* on the trail and a red one for any *colorados*. The sun had gone while he talked, but the sky was still burning bright pearl and orange.

A harsh squawk, audible above the clatter of the truck, drew our attention to a grove a way back in a pasture beside the road. A pair of macaws flew out of the grove on a course to cross the road ahead of us, complaining about some imagined ill as they flew. Blas slowed the truck to let us watch them against the flaming sky. We had seen plenty of macaws before, several pairs on this trip, but even Honduraneans seem always willing to stop to look at the big noisy creatures with their incredibly gaudy, red-yellow-and-blue plumage.

As the birds passed beyond the road their feathers caught the light, and I suddenly saw that they were not tricolored at all but one solid shade of emerald green.

"What the hell!" I yelled. "Those lapas are green. They can't be green. Green macaws have never been recorded for Honduras."

"Who hasn't recorded them?" said Blas.

La puta, said Arce, who was reared back across the mountains. "Maybe it's the light."

No fregés, hombre, said Blas in his Olancho drawl. "Remember where you are. It's not the light; it's Olancho."

PART THREE

The Sweet Sea

The Sea, the Land, and the Lake

Down in the narrowing ribbon of land that ties to-gether the continents of North and South America there is a place that has seen more than its share of history. It lies between the tenth and thirteenth parallels of latitude, and slantwise across it, northwest to southeast, there runs for two hundred miles a low, forest-filled, cloud-piled trough, barely a hundred feet above the sea — all that remains of an old way through which the Atlantic and Pacific once met and mingled. Since the dim heart of geologic time, waves and currents of life have streamed and broken and eddied about this sector of earth. It has been portal, strait, land bridge, life barrier, and highroad, and is one of the few places in the world where the ancient dramas of zoogeography have merged with the dramas of early and modern man, all moving across the same stage in continuous review.

Before the sea came through this place it had channeled the first great southward migrations of animals from northern centers of origin, and when the sea had gone it felt the back-surges of isthmian times. Across it moved the first tentative advances of new American man, fresh from the icy steppes of Asia. It saw the glory and catastrophe of a hungry Spain let loose in a new world, and through it passed the ties that a scant century ago joined the isolated halves of a new nation, just beginning to grope for one another across the northern continent.

Thirty million years ago the primal, high-raised nucleus of Middle America, now Honduras and northern Nicaragua, was a peninsula, cut off from South America by a broad connection between Atlantic and Pacific across what was to be southern Nicaragua. Also, on one or more occasions the sea cut across the upper part of the peninsula, separating it from North America; one of these straits may have coincided in time with the Nicaraguan break, making a great Middle American island, but this cannot be proved. What can be shown is that the Nicaraguan portal left South America seagirt from the equator to the antarctic and isolated from all other lands for uncounted millenniums.

The evidence by which this is known is diverse and unmistakable. The most direct proof is the presence in the Nicaraguan depression of sedimentary rocks — water-laid limestones and shales — containing fossil remains of the same warm-sea animals found in strata of the same age in the West Indies, and exposed there also. But even lacking such direct proof as this, we could still be sure that the seas met somewhere hereabout. For otherwise why should the fishes and sea turtles, and many of the spineless sea creatures of the tropical eastern Pacific, duplicate with such strange precision the faunas of the Caribbean? Not, surely, because of any intercourse over the tenuous highway around the Horn. The sameness of the shallow-water animals at Puerto Limón and Punta Arenas, at San Juan del Norte and San Juan del Sur, is almost certainly just a reflection of an old strait, long dried up when Columbus passed that way seeking the short route from Cadiz to Cathay, but there only yesterday in terms of evolutionary time.

And the proof goes even further. To the zoogeographer one look at the odd and distinctive land fauna of South America, the faunal area called Neogea, tells a story of the millions of years when the southern continent was a vast, lonely island, cut off from all the world. The hoarded biological relics, for example, could mean nothing else. The caecilians, arapaimas, and lungfishes that live on there; the seed snipes, sun bitterns, hoatzins, trumpeters, and tinamous; the world's second-largest remnant of the archaic pouched mammals; and a spectacled bear like nothing nearer than Central Asia — it was surely the sequestered peace of an island continent that let them survive. Likewise, curious new kinds of creatures were cradled there — new genera and families still confined to Neogea or just beginning to push out through the isthmian exit — electric eels and teeid lizards, wood hewers, honey creepers, hummingbirds and the special American ostrich, platyrrhine monkeys, capybaras, and a welter of ant-eaters, armadillos and sloths. All these speak of long isolation and make the South American fauna one of the curiosities of the world.

How long the seaway lasted is impossible to say even in the roundest of terms. If we knew that, our insight into the rate of evolutionary change would be much greater than it is. The most we really know is that some time toward the end of the Tertiary the bottom of the strait began to rise and spill off the sea, and growing islands and archipelagoes gradually linked the tip of the old peninsula with the southern continent. The strait squeezed shut, and among mollusks and fishes and sea turtles, brother was cut off from brother by a thousand miles of hostile shore.

Then the march of the land animals began. The pent hordes of the south were at last free to go northward, and each kind used the new freedom according to its inclination and tolerances and ability to get about. Some stayed; and some went north, only to die out in the changing climates of the Pleistocene, or to shrink back into the old security of Neogea, accompanied by wave after wave of the life of the ancient north. Back and forth they moved, up and down the narrow isthmus. Horses and camels went down, one to extinction and the other to found the llama tribe; and deer moved south and pumas after them, clear to Patagonia. Tapirs and peccaries fled before the glacial cold, and later followed the tropics back up a way. Cardinals and tanagers on their way north met the todies and motmots on their way south. The bison headed down toward the newly opened southern continent, and as far as there is any trace of its journey, stopped right at the shore of the bay that is now the Sweet Sea. The Surinam toad stayed in Surinam.

The bay where the bison stopped was an arm of the

Pacific, the eastern shore of which was formed by the high arc of the new isthmus, just eastwards of the present Nicaraguan lakes. The land bridge once rose to great heights here, but for millions of years it was wasted by erosion, and by mid-Pliocene it had been worn down to a low plain set with monadnocks along its reduced divide. Then suddenly, perhaps no more than thousands of years ago, the western floor of the bight was blasted by a line of volcanoes that appeared along the whole Pacific edge of Middle America, and the masses of lava and ash from these formed a second narrow isthmus west of the first and separated from it by the basin that now holds the great Nicaraguan lakes and their outlet, the Río San Juan.

This depression caught the runoff from the surrounding slopes and the water rose, freshening as it came up, and seeking a low place in the basin rim. The divide by now had shifted from the old isthmus to the new land bounding the trough on the west, and the water escaped across the southern end of the old divide, rising to a point some fifty feet higher than its present level and emerging near the present town of El Castillo. It flowed through the structural trough leading southeastward to the Caribbean and became the San Juan River, which, headward, cut back and down till the present outlet, several miles northwest of the original one and fifty feet lower, had been established.

The lowering of the water level in the basin cut the original lake in two — the present Lake Nicaragua and, northwest of it and connected with it across a low plain by the Río Tipitapa, the much smaller Lake Managua.

Today these two lakes, which cover forty-five hundred

of Nicaragua's forty-nine thousand square miles, and the chain of volcanoes that dammed them off make the most striking scenery that one looks down upon on the whole flight from Mexico to Panama. Lake Managua is forty-five miles long by twenty wide, and at its northern end, rising from the water on a short peninsula, is the majestic volcano with the marvelous name, Momotombo, Victor Hugo's "bald and nude colossus," and the "father of fire and stone" of the great Nicaraguan poet Rubén Darío. Momotombo is the southernmost cone in the segment of the chain of volcanoes that enters Nicaragua with Coseguïna on the Gulf of Fonseca and marches across León and Chinandega. This line and the offset file of cones that ends in the southern end of Lake Nicaragua comprise some twenty-five volcanoes in various stages of extinction; and five of them, including Momotombo, still show senile activity.

Immense and beautiful as it is, Lake Managua is a trifle compared with the inland sea south of it. For this is the Gran Lago, the Mar Dulce of the white discoverers, and the Cocibolca of the Indians before them. It is a hundred miles long and forty wide — the largest body of fresh water between Lake Michigan and Lake Titicaca, and with a lot more history behind it than either.

The water of Lake Nicaragua is fresh. It must have grown fresh gradually as the streams from the cordilleras and the new Isthmus of Rivas diluted the Pacific salt and the San Juan carried away the overflow. The lake is set with islands, all of them either volcanic cones or fragments of volcanoes scattered about by past eruptions. Neither of the lakes is very deep as big lakes go — as compared, say, to the 4,700 feet of Lake Tanganyika or the 738 feet of Lake Ontario. A maximum depth of 200 feet, occurring in a restricted area near the island of Omotepe, seems to be the deepest place in the whole system.

Besides a shower of tiny islets, nearly all of which are inhabited and cultivated, there are several sizable islands. The biggest of these is Omotepe, near the western shore, formed by two contiguous volcanoes — the still live Madera and the larger Omotepe which rises to fifty-five hundred feet above sea level and is visible all over the lake and far out in the Pacific. The island was originally inhabited by what Squier called "pure Aztecs" and its name is formed from two Nahuatl words: *ome* (two), and *tepec* (mountain). It was used by William Walker as the site of a field hospital for his filibuster troops. Isla Zapatera, which I suppose must be translated "Female Shoemaker Island," is next to Omotepe in size. It is located just south of the city of Granada. It is a famous archeological site from which large numbers of stone images and other ceremonial objects have been taken. At the southern end of the lake there is a small wooded archipelago of good-sized islands called Islas de Solentiname.

The Great Lake is bounded on the north and east by the Department of Chontales and on the west by the narrow Isthmus of Rivas. The Costa Rican frontier follows the southern boundary of the lake at a distance of two miles from it.

The chief lake port is the ancient city of Granada. Terminals of the Pacific Railroad are located at the port, which is connected by steamer service with various points about the lake shore. The most important of the other port towns are San Jorge, the port of Rivas, a city located on the western isthmus three miles from the lake shore and on the site of the old Indian capital of Nicaraocalli; and San Carlos at the outlet, where connections are made with boats that make the trip down the river to the Caribbean port of San Juan del Norte.

Lake Managua is twenty-eight feet higher than Lake Nicaragua. The Río Tipitapa, which connects the two, is sixteen miles long, and not far beyond Lake Managua there is a sixteen-foot drop in its bed which makes a respectable waterfall in the wet season. At times of low water, however, the flow is handled by underground channels and seepage, and the river disappears above this point. Just before reaching Lake Nicaragua the river broadens markedly to form a huge marshy lagoon, and its broad mouth forms the Estero de Panaloya.

Besides the overflow from Lake Managua the Great Lake receives a dozen streams that drain an immense area in the serranias of Chontales; and at the southern end there are at least ten more, including the important Río Frío from the slopes of the Costa Rican Volcan Irazú. There are four or five tributaries on the western side, noteworthy mainly because they have been surveyed as possible routes of the last leg of a transisthmian canal.

The Caribbean end of the San Juan trough is one of the rainiest places in the world, with a long-time annual average of two hundred and fifty inches and a maximum record of three hundred and forty inches. There is no severe dry season, and the rain forest extends almost over to the southern end of Lake Nicaragua, making a highway for the Atlantic rain-forest fauna that brings it closer to the Pacific shore here than anywhere else in the isthmus. The depression offers little resistance to the prevailing easterly winds, which may kick up an unpleasant chop on the lake and cause the water to pile up in one end of the basin. When the trade wind is periodically interrupted by the diurnal monsoon — the afternoon onshore breeze from the Pacific — there is a daily rise and fall of the lake water, which the ancients thought was a real tide. It was this feature of the lake as much as its great size that caused the early Spaniards to call it "El Mar Dulce." Several times each year one of the winds called *nortes* comes down. These sudden invasions of cold polar air, the continental "northers," move down the Caribbean coast and at various points may spill over the backbone cordilleras and reach the Pacific slope. In the Nicaraguan depression there is nothing to impede the strong cold winds, and, since the continental divide west of the lake is lower than at any point from Bering Strait to Patagonia, they whip across into the coastal waters of the Pacific and cause the despised squalls called *papagayos*, with reference to the Gulf of Papagayo in northern Costa Rica, where they are especially bad.

This was a pleasant place, before the Spaniards came — this land of the lake, with its blue-gold tropical air, rain washed and sun sweet — in the far past when the first brown men came down, timid and tired, to stop here and be a part of this place. Surely they had seen no such land in a thousand years of wandering. What a place to stop and rest in, after ten thousand miles of restless going! — here between the blue sea and the blue lake, in this new fertile land, fresh fed from the heart of the earth;

and the great lake spreading eastward to its inland horizon, its southern shore lost in the rain forest where spider monkeys practised their flying leaps in the bending twigs; and the howlers, with nothing else to do and nothing to dread till dark, draped themselves about to gaze at the great, slow iguanas basking on the high limbs or courting a hundred feet above water where log-long crocodiles glided in the shadows. There was high selva in the south, and on the west the clean monsoon groves with sprawling figs at the shore; and back of them great cedars and *guanacastes,* each with a trunk from which to cut a dugout to float a hundred men; and the red-and-blue macaws screaming in the exploding gold of the cortez trees; and on the flat, low shore of the north, the ironhead ibises and roseate spoonbills and all the herons walked the flats, and the limpkins poked the mud for snails; and the teal and shovelers and baldpates, the long-necked tree ducks and the big, black-and-white muscovies puddled in bog-holes or preened and slept on the floating wrack; and wine-and-lemon jaçanas postured with their poison-spined wings and sprang into short flight like angry butterflies. Two hundred miles and more of shore and no single Spaniard there, no glint of steel and no shod hoof to print the soil; and a dozen miles across the western ridge the South Sea washed the fire-dust beach; the sea snakes lolled among the floating pumice stones beyond the slow combers; the heavy sea turtles — not the land-shy males, but the old females with an errand — pounded up the shore on the young flood to keep their mindless rendezvous and nest in the alien soil; and the jaguars came down on the young flood too and walked the open beach and dug up the turtle eggs and ate them in peace, their gold-flowered sides glowing under the low moon.

The old driving rhythm of the waves was there, and the sun and the sand, and the young volcanoes roared, but no Spanish keel had creased the shore.

Hell in Paradise

ALTHOUGH the Isthmus of Rivas and the lake region generally were among the most thickly settled parts of Central America when the first white men arrived, there is a disappointing dearth of information on the people who lived there. Current anthropological studies can shed almost no light on the problem because all the tribal boundaries were disrupted and the people killed, scattered, enslaved, or crossbred during the first few years of the conquest. Bartolomé de Las Casas, whose intercession with the Spanish king checked to some extent the first ruthless abuse of the Indians, estimated that the pre-Spanish population around the great lakes was at least two million, and that this number had been reduced by three quarters within fifteen years after the discovery of the lake.

Thus, our main source of information must remain the earliest Spanish chronicles, and while these appear to furnish a fairly accurate picture of the original distribution of language stocks in the area, very little progress has been made in the correlating of the wealth of archeological material on the islands and about both lake shores with the linguistic groups found by the discoverers. It is frustrating to a layman to find that nobody knows who really made the big statues from Zapatera. It must be worse to the anthropologists working with the problem.

The Indians whom Gil González found in northern Costa Rica during the march that led to the discovery of the Great Lakes were the Corobici, a tribe of the Talamancan Division, and the same people who later moved to the upper reaches of the Río Frío, where they became known as the Guatusos and were much feared by the inhabitants of the lake shore. The Talamancan Division was also represented by the Rama tribe of Chontales and the Caribbean slope, who were mostly confined to the rivers draining northward, but who may have reached the southeastern shore of Lake Nicaragua from time to time. Northward of Rama territory lived the Ulvas, a tribe of the Sumo river-Indians of the Caribbean Lowland Division.

All the rest of the territory around the lakes, including the islands and the heavily populated Isthmus of Rivas, was held by expatriate Mayans and by Mexicans — the various kinds of Chorotegans and the more recently arrived Nahuas, represented by the powerful tribe ruled by the chief Nicarao, and usually referred to by his name. These latter people are believed to have reached the isthmus as late as A.D. 1000. The only other Nahuatlan group to come down was a small tribe living in the area between the Great Lakes. They spoke Aztec, but what they called themselves is forgotten.

The Chorotegans represented the earliest southward migration of the so-called Meso-American people. There were three tribes of them: the Nagrandians at the northern end of Lake Managua, the Dirians seaward of the Aztec country in the base of the western isthmus, and along the western shore of Lake Managua the Mangues, from whose name that of the lake must have been put together as "Mangue-agua" and then contracted, paralleling the etymology of "Nicaraoagua" for Lake Cocibolca.

These are the people who felt the fury of the first bands of hidalgos, hyperthyroid by breeding, hog-poor and callous to human agony from almost a thousand years of fighting Moors in their own wrecked land; and the despair of the Sweet Sea people was hardly equalled in all the ages till the cunning of our own times made it seem trivial.

It is not known how soon after the final closure of the Nicaraguan portal the precursors of these men joined the parade of animals into and out of the southern continent and the first Nicaraguans settled about the lake shore. Recent discoveries showing that men in South America lived among animals now extinct; the extension of the ice age calendar by evidence from radioactive carbon; and such odds and ends of data as the surprising occurrence of bison hoofprints among the human footprints in the clearly ancient fossil trails of Cahualinca near Managua — all these tend to push back the history of Middle American man, who, it seems reasonable to guess, may have lived near the shore of the old Nicaraguan Bay before the volcanic barrier cut it off and built the Sweet Sea.

The drainage system of the Great Lakes was first seen by white men in 1502, when Columbus passed the mouth of the outlet close inshore on his fourth voyage. His caravels had just been through the ordeal of a Honduranean *temporal:* for twenty-eight days of torment they had beaten through driving rain into a furious southeaster that made the Admiral's stubborn clinging to the coast line seem like madness. But he stayed inshore; and on September 14 he passed a headland that let him change his course and run off the wind. The relief he felt is clear in the name he gave the cape: Gracias a Dios.

This time Columbus was looking for the secret strait, the passage to the Indian Sea; he clung fiercely to the low shore while his gaze swept the blue hills back of it for the break that hope told him would loose his caravels to the setting sun and to the jewels of Samarkand, and him to immortality.

But he was too late. Too late by twenty million years at least. An epoch earlier a narrow bridge of land had shuffled off the sea and blocked the passage; the strait was only a king's dream that no ship would ever ride. And when in the third week of September the Admiral passed the mouth of the Desaguadero, the outlet of the great fresh lake hidden over against the shore of the South Sea, he had no way of knowing that this was the nearest thing to a strait he would find that side of Tierra del Fuego. There was nothing about the gap in the flat swampy shore to lure his ships into the waterway that twenty years later would bear frigates of almost twice the burden of the little *Capitana* back and forth to the Sweet Sea and its western shore, a morning's walk from the Pacific.

103

I wonder how the mad story of the Conquest would have gone if Columbus had seen the Desaguadero for what it was. But the river gave no sign that it came down from Mahomet's Paradise; and the tough old Admiral coasted on toward Panama, easing his grief over the lost secret of the strait with the *guañín* gold of Coriay, and sailing home to die.

This did not end the search for the westward passage. Eighteen years later Carlos V was still uneasy over the thought that Columbus could have missed it, and this hope more than anything else led to the discovery and conquest of the lake region of Nicaragua. The passage that the Portuguese Ferdinand Magellan had found in 1520, down past the bleak tip of the unknown world beyond Tierra Firme, was too far to call a passage really, and there must be something better, hidden perhaps by a re-curved headland or in the lee of a longshore key or island. Thus, in 1521, with Mexico and Peru conquered, Cortés in the north and Pedrárias in Panama were ordered to push the search for a seaway somewhere in the land be-tween them.

It was at this time that Gil González Dávila sailed from Panama to the Gulf of Nicoya, landed with one hundred men and four horses, and made his way into the territory of the cacique Nicoya, who received him amiably and told him of a great lake to the north. Gil's chaplain bap-tized Nicoya, and they pushed on northward. After fight-ing their way through heavy swamp, they arrived at the western shore of the great lake called Cocibolca by the people there, who were ruled by the powerful cacique Nicarao.

In all his dealings with the Indians Gil González had
two potent allies: his horses and the beards of his men.
The latter so awed the Indians and smoothed the path of
conquest that Gil ordered twenty-five smooth-faced members of the party to wear false beards made from the hair
of their heads.

Chief Nicarao admitted the Spaniards to his court at
Nicaraocalli, *capital de cacicazgo,* from near which Gil
saw the vast spread of Lake Cocibolca, and this fanned
the flame of his faith in the hidden strait. Chief Nicarao,
unable to foresee the misery that would follow these white
men into his land, allowed himself to be baptised along
with nine thousand of his people, but only after cross-
catechizing the priests in a way that embarrassed them
considerably. After that he gave the Spaniards presents
of gold and plumes and raiment to the value of twenty-
five thousand pieces of eight. Gil rewarded his generosity
with a cloth cap, a shirt, and some amulets and children's
jewelry.

The Spaniards learned that the Great Lake had an outlet which flowed into the North Sea. They were also told
that there was a connection with Lake Xolotlán (Managua) and that this in turn flowed into the southern sea.
To Gil this was his chance for undying glory, and he hur-
ried forward to reconnoiter the long-sought seaway. He
found a great bay called then Chorotega and now the
Gulf of Fonseca. Here some of the people confirmed the
stories of a connection with Xolotlán, while others claimed
that there was a direct passage across the isthmus from
Chorotega to the Gulf of Honduras. Gil was too excited
to be critical. He rushed back to Panama full of news. He

was coldly received by Pedrárias, who was jealous over the supposed success of the venture, and who with Spanish logic refused to recognize that Gil had found anything because he had not gone with proper authority to look for a strait. Lacking support in Panama, Gil went off to Santo Domingo to begin an involved and heartbreaking campaign for recognition that ended only when he returned to Spain and died in 1526.

Meantime, Pedrárias outfitted an expedition under the doughty Andalusian Francisco Hernández de Córdoba, the explorer of Yucatan, with a hand-picked army of Andalusian soldiers to take for him Gil González' *Paraíso de Mahoma*, as it now was beginning to be called. After reaching the lake and making an alliance with Nicarao, Hernández marched on toward the head of the lake into the country of the Dirians, and on the site of a town called Jalteba, capital of the chief Nequecheri, built the city of Granada, naming it after the metropolis of his native Andalusia. He raised a fort on the lake shore, built the magnificent church of San Francisco, which is still standing, and hauled overland on the backs of Nicarao's people the pieces of a brigantine which he put together on the lake for a voyage of exploration.

The first reconnaissance of the Mar Dulce was made by Captain Rui Dias, who found the Desaguadero, as they now called the outlet, and explored it as far as the first rapids.

Hernández sent a second party to explore the outlet, under command of Hernando de Soto, already a lord of the Inca Empire and to become at last Adelantado of Florida and find a grave in the Mississippi. But de Soto did little better than Dias, only reaching a point near the

river-bank settlement of Voto a little above the rapids of
El Toro.

At about this time the old Indian name for the lake,
"Cocibolca" — the Mar Dulce of the first conquistadores —
began to be replaced in the writings of the scribes by the
hybrid combination "Nicaraoagua," which was eventually contracted to "Nicaragua" and applied to the whole
country.

The royal instructions to the first governors of Nicaragua were "to continue the exploration of the river, and
to determine whether it was navigable as far as the sea
and whether it and the lake afforded a passage from one
sea to another." As a base for operations on the river the
cruel Governor Diego López de Salcedo established the
town of Nuevo Jaen on the eastern shore of the lake between the Tepenaguasapa and Oyate rivers. Of this place
no trace remains. Pedrárias, who replaced the tyrannical
Salcedo with a rule quite as insanely sadistic, sent down
the river an exploring expedition under Martín Estete,
but this was soon stopped by abnormally low water over
the rocks.

It was not until 1539 that the mouth of the river was
discovered. In that year the governor Rodrigo de Con-
treras, son-in-law of Pedrárias, organized an exploring
party under the joint leadership of Alonso Caleras and
Diego Machuca, with a fleet of two sailing scows, two
cayucas, and a ship with a "deck over the stern and under
this forty horses and a pen of pigs." One of these vessels
was called the "San Juan," and it seems likely that the
river took from it the name Río San Juan which came into
use at this time. At the El Toro rapids Machuca, whose

name is today borne by another rapids in the river, took the horses and a small group of men and proceeded over-land in search of the mouth of the river, losing himself completely in the trackless selvas and winding up far to the north at Río Coco, where he had to eat his horses and return to Granada on foot. Caleras eventually reached the sea, but unaccountably took it for another great lake until a storm sank three of his ships and reduced his party to seven survivors.

In 1578 three ships of war and a launch were built in the Great Lake and used to descend the river and consoli-date a route out to Cartagena, Havana, and Cadiz — the strange, unlikely route down through the rain forest of San Juan, where frigates would soon go bumping over the rocks and make a rich and busy Caribbean port of a city tucked away back inside the isthmus, within spitting dis-tance of the "Indian Sea." Granada was to become a great seaport and a vital link with Spain.

For some time the Spaniards had been deviled by pi-rates, mostly stray Hollanders or Englishmen, who sneaked in to slash at the *flota* or the *galeones* and then ran like gulls. It was really the pirates that brought wealth to Granada, although the unhappy city paid it back with ruinous interest. During the last decade of the sixteenth century the menace had grown, and the old lanes from the Gulf of Honduras and Nombre de Dios were no longer safe. A new way out had to be found, where a quick dash in the open sea to Cartagena might elude the buccaneers. The only new way there was went down through the for-est from the Great Lake, and for a few decades the trade and revenue of Central America passed through Granada and the lake and the Río San Juan. During the first quarter of the seventeenth century a fleet of *frigadas*, ships of well over a hundred-ton burden, regularly made the river passage with little inconvenience; and during this time the only rapids that seems to have impeded traffic was that to which the name of the explorer Captain Machuca had been given. Over the hundred-mile length of the river the outgoing frigates were safe from the buccaneers, and just before reaching the river mouth, small boats were sent ahead to reconnoiter the coast. It was inevitable that the great pirate strongholds of Bluefields and Pearl Lagoon should grow up to prey on the Granada frigates.

Granada had her worries. Long before this the terrible Drake had threaded his way through the Straits of Magellan to harry the ships and ports of the southern shore. Drake prowling off the southern shore of Paradise, looking lustfully across Rivas and into the very Sweet Sea itself, where the cones of Omotepe rose as a beacon to pirate or friend alike, must have brought discomfort to Granada. But it would know worse.

By the time Thomas Gage, the "English American" Dominican friar, arrived in Granada to take a ship to Spain and end his extraordinary *vuelta* in the new world, the passage down the San Juan had become hard for seagoing ships. Whether the series of earthquakes that eventually made it necessary to transship all river cargo to flatboats had begun to affect the channel before Gage got there is not known, but something had happened to the river. Gage was at once impressed by the stature of this inland port city and disturbed at his poor prospects for getting early passage from what he called the "Paradise of America" back to Europe. His account gives a unique picture of the Granada of that time:

> ... at this time of the sending away of the frigates that town is one of the wealthiest in all the north tract of America; for the merchants of Guatemala, fearing to send all their goods by the Gulf of Honduras for that they have been often taken by the Hollanders between that and Havana, think it safer to send them by the frigates to Cartagena.... So likewise many times the King's treasure and revenues (when there is any report of ships at sea or about St. Anthony) are in this way by the Lake of Granada passed to Cartagena.

He told of the arrival in Granada in one day of six mule trains — a total of three hundred mules — laden with indigo, cochineal, and hides from Guatemala and Comayagua, and "two days after from Guatemala came in three more, the one laden with silver [which was the king's tribute from that country]. . . ." He characteristically made the most of his delay and took his pleasure up and down the country, where he "was much feasted by the Mercedarian friars who enjoy most of those towns" and who gave him dismal reports of the journey down the river:

> For whilst they [the frigates] sail upon the lake they go securely and without trouble, yet when they fall from the lake to the river to go out to sea ... here is nothing but trouble ... for such is the fall of the water among the rocks that many times they are forced to unlade the frigates and lade them again....

When at last the ship on which Gage had arranged passage was on the eve of departure, there suddenly came "a strict command from Guatemala that the frigates should not go out that year, because the President ... was informed for certain that some English or Holland ships was abroad at sea, and lay about the mouth of the Desaguadero waiting for the frigates of Granada. . . ."

By 1663, when the last of several earthquakes believed to have raised the bed of the river occurred, seagoing traffic was virtually at an end. A big Cuban ship caught in the lake was sold for her timber and hardware at public auction. Granada was no longer a deepwater seaport, and the Sweet Sea no longer an arm of the Caribbean.

But the four bad rapids in the river were not enough to keep out the world. In 1665 the pirate Edward Hume with a hundred and forty men went up the river in dugouts, and at two o'clock in the morning of June 29 sacked and burned Granada. The worst part of this raid was not the fire or the looting but the publicity it brought, for it called attention to the vulnerability as well as to the strategic location of the Great Lake, and loosed upon Mahomet's Paradise the greed and ambition of the world. Up until now the misery of the Isthmus of Rivas had been its own affair and of its own doing, but now the place was wide open and sure to become a stage for world strife.

Efforts were made to fortify the entrance to the lake, but these could not keep pace with the forces assaulting it. In 1666 a defensive tower was erected at El Castillo on the upper reaches of the river, and huge rocks were dumped into the rapids there to offer further obstruction to the invaders everyone knew would come fast now. Forts were placed at the mouths of two tributary streams. A tax was levied to finance the building of a fort at San Carlos by the mouth of the outlet on the lake shore. The fact that this tax schedule included a levy of fifty pieces of eight for "each frigate that left for Spain" (as well as two reales for each mule that left for Panama) implies that the river was still used by ocean-going craft, but these were almost surely trundled empty through the rapids and their cargoes portaged. The defenses at San Carlos were finished in 1667. In 1685 Granada was burned the second time by l'Olonnois, who came over from the Pacific side; and in 1690 the pirate Gallardillo captured the new fort and raided several points about the lake. This violence prompted the building of the famous Castillo de la Imaculada Concepción at the Santa Cruz Rapids on the San Juan and the fortifying of eight more sites on the lower river.

With this the pirates were held off for a time, but they loafed about the North Coast and the lean years began for Nicaragua.

When Edward Hume sacked Granada he made a remark to the elders of the city which forecast the period of disaster that the country would now enter. He said that he valued as but the price of a bottle of wine all the loot of Granada in comparison with the privilege of having seen the city and the lake with its *isletas* and the island of Omotepe; and he vowed to do everything in his power to persuade either the English or the Portuguese to give him men, ships, and arms to take and hold the ports of the lake from which a connection with the South Sea could so easily be made.

It may be that this was the germ of the idea of a transisthmian canal in the Nicaraguan trough, the idea of digging the strait no one could find. At any rate, from about this time on until the United States began to resent her action England took over the persecution of Nicaragua on an official level, and the complex, unlikely stories of her maneuverings, ending with the creation of the fantastic Mosquito Kingdom to guard for the Empire the entrance to the San Juan Valley and the best canal route in the isthmus, have been the subjects of a shelf of books.

In 1762 English overtures in Nicaragua gave the country a national heroine. An English fleet of fifty ships and two thousand men ascended the river and attacked the fort at El Castillo shortly after the Nicaraguan commander there had died. When a sergeant left in charge of the garrison seemed on the point of surrendering the fort to the enemy, Rafaela Herrera, the nineteen-year-old daughter of the dead officer, grabbed the linstock and fired the cannon herself, with such good effect that the third shot killed the English commander and sank a sloop. When night fell and darkness hid the English fleet, Rafaela soaked some sheets in alcohol, piled them on rafts, set them afire, and had them thrown into the river, where the current carried them down upon the English ships. This not only illuminated the target for fire from the batteries of Castillo, but scared the wits out of the Englishmen, who thought Greek fire had been loosed on them, and who retreated in confusion and eventually gave up the siege. The girl was celebrated in Granada and throughout the kingdom of Guatemala, and the Spanish crown awarded her a lifetime pension for her heroic service.

The first survey of the river and lake as a possible canal way was made in 1781 by the Spanish engineer Manuel Galisteo. Toward the end of the North American Revolution, Spain joined the war on the side of the American colonists and the French, and tried to drive the British from their holdings on the mainland of Honduras and Nicaragua. In 1779 England sent a big expedition to Central America for the purpose of protecting her colonies and of cutting Spanish America in two by gaining control of Lake Nicaragua. Horatio Nelson accompanied this party as a post captain, and it was on this trip that he lost his eye.

Old Cocibolca was by now being called an inland Gibraltar and another Mediterranean, and not again for over a century would it cease to be in the eyes of the world. The British expedition was successful in a military way, but the yellow fever and malaria of the river bottoms took a ghastly toll of the redcoats, seamen, and marines. El Castillo was captured on April 2, 1780, but of Nelson's garrison of five hundred only ten survived.

During most of the first half of the nineteenth century England had a free hand in Nicaragua, opposed, before the liberation of 1821, only by the distraught Spanish, and thereafter by no one. But during the 1840's, when the acquisition of California by the United States had pushed the western frontier to the Pacific, powerful forces began to converge in Nicaragua and to make of it one of the hottest spots in the whole world. For now the sad little country, besides being torn by almost continuous civil war, and besides having the misfortune to hold a canal route coveted by the marine powers of the world, found itself sitting astride the slender line of communication between the two segregated parts of the rowdy new nation to the north.

In 1814 von Humboldt had disproved the old superstition that a difference in level of the Caribbean and Pacific would make an isthmian canal impracticable, and with Spain shortly out of the field the scramble began. First the United States and then the Dutch made false starts toward planning a canal; then in 1846 Louis Napoleon published a pamphlet called *Canal in Nicaragua*, which put everyone into a sweat over the Sweet Sea and its potential place in the commerce of the world.

"There exists in the New World," said Napoleon, writing in English, "a state as admirably situated as Constantinople, and, we must say, up to this time as uselessly occupied. We allude to the state of Nicaragua. As Constantinople is the center of the ancient world, so is the town of León the center of the new, and if the tongue of land which separates its two lakes from the Pacific Ocean were cut through, she would command by virtue of her central position, the entire coast of North and South America. The state of Nicaragua can become, better than Constantinople, the necessary route of the great commerce of the world, and is destined to attain an extraordinary degree of prosperity and grandeur."

This tract caused a sensation. England, fearing its effects on the rest of the world, at once began moving to protect her interests in the San Juan valley, taking San Juan del Norte (Greytown) in the name of the Mosquito King and in 1849 wangling from Nicaragua the Agreement of the Isla de Cuba (an island in the lake), which recognized the puppet Kingdom of Mosquitia on all the Caribbean North Coast.

Then came the forty-niners, streaming through the

trough, hot after California gold and the quickest way to get at it. Cornelius Vanderbilt came down too, not on his way to Sutter's Mill but with a scheme that mined California gold all the same by moving the forty-niners across the isthmus. George Squier, first United States minister to Nicaragua, arrived and squabbled with the British and brought on a crisis that blew over, but that left a lot of bad blood.

In 1850 Vanderbilt's interoceanic transit company began to operate. The Caribbean terminus was San Juan del Norte, which boomed and became the first of that handful of Caribbean port towns that have probably equalled any in the world for pure hell-raising ribaldry. Passengers and freight from ships of the Commodore's own line were here transferred to the river steamboat *Director*, a 120-ton ship built in New York by J. Simonson. The *Director* carried four hundred passengers and seventy tons of coal, and the name of its captain was Samuel Leighton. It ran up the river as far as El Castillo, where it made connections with another steamer, the *Nicaragua*, and this completed the trip up the river and across the lake to the port of La Virgen on the western shore. From here a line of blue-and-white stagecoaches crossed the fourteen-mile Isthmus of Rivas and met the California ships at the port of San Juan del Sur.

In 1854 William Walker, the gray-eyed man from Tennessee, arrived in the full flush of his paranoia, fresh from his Sonoran fiasco but still burning with faith in himself as crusader for manifest destiny. He had chosen Nicaragua as the scene of his crimes because the perennial civil war there offered the chance for him to get into the thick of

national affairs without delay. Almost at once he got the
glory he craved. He became general in the Liberal army,
and then made himself president of Nicaragua, and his
exploits held the incredulous attention of the world.

During this time Nicaragua was tossed about on the rip
where four fierce contrary currents met. There was the
demented Walker, the puritanical killer with his personal
ambition; there were the maneuverings of the financial
filibuster Vanderbilt, blood enemy of Walker and as ruthless, in more legal ways; there was England, still with a
bulldog grip on her canal claims; and there was the United
States of the North, growing, spreading westward like the
cytoplasm of an ameba streaming out to fill a drawn-out
thread of itself, breasting the melee in the isthmus, re-
inforcing the confusion. This was the maddest time in the
history of any of the torn republics of Latin America, and
its climax and denouement left unhurt only the ornery old
Commodore, whose millions were at last the strongest
force of all.

In 1854 the United States shook the confidence of Spanish America and came close to war with England when
it ordered the naval bombardment of San Juan del Norte,
on the pretext that our consul there had been mistreated,
but actually in a fit of temper with the Anglo-Mosquito
officials holding the port. The situation that led to this
perverse move was engineered by Vanderbilt, whose
transit concession the presence of the British in San Juan
del Norte seemed to threaten. William Walker should
have taken heed of this sign of the Commodore's power,
but as usual his delusions dulled his foresight, and he proceeded to cross and alienate the financier at every turn.

When Vanderbilt's patience gave out, he simply closed the transit line to the north and cut off the California steamer service. This quickly throttled Walker by depriving him of supplies and of the American recruits who had been the backbone of his forces. His star began to set at once, his glory faded fast, and in 1856 his incredible career ended at Trujillo before a firing squad of scared and barefoot Honduraneans.

The first American survey of the San Juan depression as a possible canal route was made by Vanderbilt in 1852, who probably never had any real idea of digging a canal, but whose transit company rights were secured as part of a concession for a canal route that Squier had negotiated. The survey was apparently made merely to conciliate Nicaragua, and its results were favorable.

The results of most of the many surveys made in Nicaragua were favorable — more consistently so than in the case of any of the several other transisthmian routes that have been studied, including Panama. Why, then, was the lake route not the one chosen when in 1902 the United States finally committed itself to dig a canal across the isthmus? If there is any one simplest answer, it is volcanoes — volcanoes, and one of the shrewdest and most relentless lobbies that ever swayed an American Congress.

The lobby was engineered by three men: Senator Mark Hanna, William Nelson Cromwell — a brilliant corporation lawyer with a financial stake in Panama — and the French propagandist Philippe Jean Bunau-Varilla, whose principal motive seems to have been the desire to vindicate the engineering genius of his countrymen, who had long been scratching away at the Panama route. Deftly channeled and exploited to the full by Bunau-Varilla, the single factor which at the very last turned Congress from the long preferred Nicaraguan route was fear of Momotombo and its fellows, most of them long dead but still good propaganda.

The lobby had gained a potent psychological advantage when on May 6 the news arrived of the terrible eruption of Mt. Pelee, which killed twenty-five thousand people in St. Pierre, Martinique, in the worst natural disaster of modern times.

On May 13 there came notice of an eruption of Momotombo said to have wrecked some docks and buildings on the shore of Lake Managua. Bunau-Varilla nosed out a Nicaraguan postage stamp with a picture of a smoking volcano on it. He bought up a large number of these and to every member of Congress he sent one, pasted dramatically in the center of a sheet of paper. *The New York Sun* joined the campaign for Panama and gave the lobby editorial support with this menacing letter from Momotombo to the opposition:

My compliments to Senator Morgan [John T. Morgan of Alabama, who had fought for a canal for years and at the time favored the Nicaraguan way]. I beg leave to inform that gentleman and others whom it may concern that I am not only alive but am capable of sending down, without notice, through Lake Managua and the Tipitapa River into the adjacent Lake Nicaragua a tidal wave of sufficient volume and malignity to overwhelm any canal that engineering skill can construct through this country and to wipe out every dollar of the two or three hundred million which the United States Government may be foolish enough to invest in the waters subject to my power. Precisely the same thing can be done, and with equally

119

short notice, by my neighbors and allies, Pilas, Nindiri, Telica, Santa Clara, Oros, Isla Venado, Fernando Mancaron, Mancaroncita, Madera, Omotepe, and the Hell of Masaya — any one of them or all combined.

Under this pressure Congress suddenly stopped brooding over the advantages of the route through Nicaragua, and on June 2, 1902, passed the Spooner Bill that authorized the Panama Canal.

But the Sweet Sea passage has not been forgotten. The file is hauled out every now and then, especially when wartime makes the idea of a spare canal attractive and the nearness of Nicaragua becomes a vital factor.

The most recent survey was made from 1929 to 1931 by a battalion of United States Army Engineers, commanded by Lieutenant Colonel Dan I. Sultan, and working under the direction of the Interoceanic Canal Board, composed of two army engineers and three civilian engineers. This survey agreed with that of 1852, both in its favorable evaluation of the route and in most of the details of the course advised. The Caribbean entrance to the canal would be the mouth of the Río Deseado, just north of the San Juan delta. It would follow the Deseado for fifteen miles and then cut over to the San Juan and run with the general trend of its bed all the way up to Lake Nicaragua. It would cross the lake to the mouth of the Río Las Lajas, which drains the center of the Isthmus of Rivas, follow this to the divide, and there cut through to the Pacific at the port of Brito. The route would be about one hundred seventy-three miles long, nearly three and a half times as long as the Panama Canal; but Panama's deepest cut (Culebra) is one hundred fifty feet deeper than any that the lake route would require. As in Panama, the differences in level would be handled by three locks at either end. The survey estimated the time necessary to complete the canal as ten years and the cost as $720,000,000. The former would probably be less today and the latter surely a great deal more.

The bandit patriot Sandino opposed the 1929 survey and boasted that he would cut off the heads of the men sent to make it, but nothing came of this. For some reason most Nicaraguans, who more than any of our Latin neighbors have reason to mistrust the United States, seem to like us. When in other parts of Nicaragua a few gringo heads actually did roll under *sandinista* machetes, there was no way of knowing how much secret satisfaction spread through the land, but I have a notion that rejoicing would have been more general in many other countries.

Throughout our century of intervention in Nicaragua the good nature of the people there has been the only stable factor in the relationship. The patience of Nicaragua, bred by the hidalgos and nurtured by the pirates, the English, the filibusters, and the chronic pain of endless civil war, has weathered now a full hundred years of petulant and inconsistent treatment by the United States. Our shelling of San Juan del Norte; our tardy and half-hearted repudiation of the mad Walker; our alarming faith in Manifest Destiny and the Big Stick; the pious persecutions of Dollar Diplomacy and fiscal intervention; our landings of Marines and the uncontrolled excesses of our wartime good-will propaganda — all these, though well remembered, are to an astonishing degree forgiven us.

On the whole, the Nicos like us and the gringo stamp is

on the country. In the familiar, family-album look of the
Marine-trained national guard you see it, and in the blue-
eyed mestizos, strangely stratified in age-groups, marking
the towns where the Marines stopped; in the old jazz-
age tunes, half buried and overgrown by the Andalusian
rhythms and Indian scale changes of the guitars of Mata-
galpa, and audible to no gringo under forty; in the universal, now almost hereditary, excellence of Nicaraguan
baseball and in its umpire's jargon bridging the gaps that
Esperanto and Basic English never crossed. If these are
heelmarks of an oppressor they are not seen as such. In
spite of ourselves, we have a steadfast good neighbor in
the land around the Sweet Sea, and when the time comes
to dig the strait the old Admiral never found, we shall be
among friends.

The Red Fishes

THE thing that first drew my attention to the Nicaraguan lakes was not among those things I have been talking about. It was the fishes that live in them. In the two Great Lakes — Managua and Nicaragua — ichthyologists have recognized and named about thirty-five kinds of fishes. While this number is considerably higher than that for Lake Yojoa in Honduras, Atitlán in Guatemala, or Chapala in Mexico, it is not enough to cause any special excitement over the mere diversity of the fauna.

But there are some exciting things about the fishes of the Sweet Sea. For besides the list of kinds that any fish expert might predict for this combination of locality, drainage, and altitude, there are in these lakes: (a) landlocked sea fishes, (b) red fishes, and (c) butt-headed fishes; and about each of these there are certain things that are hard to understand or interesting to contemplate.

The marine fishes, which have not been found in Lake

Managua but only in Nicaragua, are a shark, a sawfish, and the common widespread tarpon. Looking back to the history that has been ascribed to the Mar Dulce — the cutting off of an arm of the sea by volcanic damming — it might not seem too surprising that some of the inhabitants of the old bay should have managed to adapt themselves to the age-long fall in salinity and hang on in the fresh lake of today. But this line of reasoning gets nowhere, because the bay was almost certainly cut off from the Pacific — not from the Caribbean — while the shark is clearly most closely related to the ordinary cub shark of the Atlantic side. Not only that, but the tarpon is evidently plain old *Tarpon atlanticus,* whose antics on a line and shine in the sun lure the rich Yankees down to Boca Grande and Brownsville and Tampico, and which ranges the Atlantic shores from Cape Cod to Brazil but never gets into the Pacific at all. The sawfish is a kind that could be from nearly anywhere. Not much is known about sawfishes, and the lake population could just as well have come from one ocean as the other.

Thus we have the apparent anomaly of an impounded arm of the Pacific, now separated from its mother sea by only twelve miles of dry land, but with a fish fauna in which two salt-water species are obviously derived from the Caribbean a hundred miles away.

But the situation is not so bad as it looks. A little meditation on the recorded past of the Caribbean approach to the Great Lake suggests a solution to the problem: the fishes came up the San Juan River before the rapids formed.

The relatives of all three of the Sweet Sea relicts are

what ecologists call euryhaline species — that is, they are able to take changes in the salinity of their environment as they come — and they are characteristically found wandering into brackish estuaries and even into the fresh streams tributary to these. A few years ago some kind of shark was killed at Branford, Florida, away back toward the middle of the peninsula, where the Suwannee River is fresh as rain. Tarpon prowl all about the edges of the Everglades in rainwater runoff, and the most tarpon I ever saw in one place cruised past our camp on a Nicaraguan river from which all our drinking water came.

It must be significant too that the very species of shark from which the lake *tiburón* is obviously derived (*Carcharhinus leucas*), and from which it differs only in a few trivial features, is well known for its long excursions up fresh rivers. It has turned up in several Nicaraguan streams, and one specimen was taken one hundred eighty miles up the Patuca in Honduras. Moreover, the lake form still clings to its love of a current in its face and has been found far up the Río Frío, the big, cold stream that comes down to the Sweet Sea from the high volcanoes of Costa Rica.

There are two distractors that got visiting zoologists started thinking of these fishes as Pacific relicts and that keep people around the lakes thinking of them as such: the remoteness of the Caribbean as compared to the nearness of the southern shore, and the furious rapids that bar the passage up the San Juan at four places. The first of these factors may be set aside at once as of no concern to such rovers as the cub shark and the tarpon. And it seems very probable that the rapids, also, can be discounted as a barrier to fish migrants, since in their present form they are almost surely not much more than three hundred years old. As we have seen earlier, the old writers spoke of regular commercial shipping from Granada and the lake ports directly to Spain, Cuba, and Cartagena. This service was carried on by frigates with a burden of between eighty and one hundred twenty tons, and until the 1630's, when the first of a series of earthquakes began blocking the channel, the ships ran all the way up to the lake with no portaging of cargo. Where a clumsy frigate went, a shark or tarpon — or for that matter even a sawfish — surely could have gone, and while they are evidently landlocked in the lake today, they probably came and went at will before the rapids built up.

The curious thing to me is that all the demands of all the stages in the life cycles of the creatures should have been met by the waters of the lake. While the breeding habits of the lake tarpon are no better known than those of its salt-water relative, there can be little doubt that it produces young in the lake, and there is no doubt at all about the shark and the sawfish, because they are often caught pregnant and in the excitement of being landed have their pups right in the boat as their sisters in the sea so often do. That is the unique aspect of these animals; they are the only ones of their kind anywhere in the world that have become permanently and completely adjusted to living in fresh water, finding all their food there, and breeding and producing young that grow to maturity.

When the lake shark lost contact with its marine relatives, four things happened to it: the position of its eyes shifted slightly, its gill openings enlarged by a trifle, the free tip of its second dorsal fin grew longer, and its disposition got worse. Of all these points of divergence the last is by far the most striking. For while nobody has ever proved that the cub shark attacks people, its Sweet Sea counterpart is a genuinely ornery beast which, even making allowances for the demoralizing effect sharks have on the keepers of records, has almost certainly been responsible for the death and injury of numerous persons and of uncounted hordes of dogs. The authors of the best shark book available, Henry Bigelow and William Schroeder, who are very conservative and reliable yankeemen and as slow as anybody to malign a shark unjustly, have this to say on the subject:

> It is reputedly dangerous to bathers, as well as to any dog that may venture into the lake. And published accounts of its ferocity appear to be well founded, for a correspondent in whom we have full confidence reports that he has not only seen an attack on a youth swimming at San Carlos, but has heard of actual fatalities at other localities around the lake. Very recently the press has reported attacks on bathers and fishermen at Granada, where one of the victims lost an arm, while another lost his right leg and had his left leg injured.

Luis Marden, who got to know the Great Lakes *tiburones* well in 1943, when he caught and photographed them and discussed with numerous lake fishermen their capacity for mayhem, believed that at least one person is killed each year on the lake by sharks.

The average length of the lake species appears to be about six feet, and individuals of this length weigh around one hundred fifty pounds. This is not big as sharks go, and since marine species very rarely attack man until they reach lengths of nine or ten feet or more and can practically demolish him at a bite, the ferocity of the limb-clipping landlocked breed is the more striking.

Nicaraguans are immensely proud of their fresh-water shark. The only material benefits it brings them are soup-fins for the Chinese of Granada and Managua and a trickle of vitamin oil from a feeble fishery, but that doesn't matter; and even the fact that it chews them up from time to time has engendered admiration for the spirit of the animal more than resentment. The fishermen of Lake Nicaragua look down on those of Lake Managua because they have no shark in their lake, and the Managua fishermen are quite sensitive about it.

A lake full of tarpon, sawfish that get to weigh seven hundred pounds, and a landlocked shark that eats people make quite a show in themselves, but they are not the only arresting feature of the fauna of the Mar Dulce. The cichlid fishes are, in their way, every bit as interesting.

The cichlids are a family of small to medium-sized fishes, much like our sunfishes in general appearance — some deep-bodied like bluegills and others similar to bass in size and shape. The family has a curious world distribution, being known from Central and South America and from Africa. In the old lakes of the African rift valley, Tanganyika and Nyasa, the cichlids have undergone a riot of evolutionary activity that has no parallel among backboned animals unless it be the honey creepers of Hawaii. In Lake Nyasa these fishes, perhaps egged on by competition set up when several closely related stocks found themselves together in the same body of water, have split up and subdivided to the most unbelievable extent and have produced what are known as species flocks — swarms of microspecies — each of which breeds only with its own kind and yet is distinguished from scores of fellow species only by some fussy little detail of structure of the mouth or pharynx. In one Nyasa genus it is possible to lay out over a hundred species that hardly anyone could tell apart without looking in their mouths. It is almost as if someone should set out a row of a hundred crappies or yellow perch and tell you there were a hundred different kinds there.

The Nicaraguan cichlids show some slight tendency toward this sort of thing, but it is not marked. There are eighteen kinds known from the two lakes, and it is quite possible that some of these are composites of two or more species not yet distinguished. This is a larger list than could be counted in any area of similar size in the new world. Moreover, of these eighteen kinds, all but one are endemic — that is to say, are found nowhere else in the world. Furthermore, among these species there are some clusters of forms so very similar that their differing at all seems mere irresponsible caprice, annoying to the fish student and of no earthly use to the fish.

But on the whole the Nyasa cichlids far outdo the Nicaraguan ones in their keen eye for nuances of adaptive evolution. It is a very different sort of thing that sets the Sweet Sea cichlids apart. It is a tendency for some of the perfectly distinct and evidently only distantly related species there to show two of the same bizarre variations — a grotesque high hump on the forehead and a color phase of golden red.

The first thing I ever heard of the red fishes of the Nicaraguan lakes was the remark I came across in Stout's

Nicaragua, which I read when I was living in Honduras. "The lake," Stout said, "is full of goldfish, which we can see distinctly finning along, their gleaming scales relieved by the white sand bottom."

He was not talking about Lake Nicaragua but about Lake Apoya, a small lake five miles from Granada. I remember taking his remark as a flight of fancy, since Stout was a poetical sort of fellow who went on to describe the place where he saw the goldfish as "calm, clear, beautiful — the embodiment, the realization of Bulwer's 'Lake of Como,' where every floating cloudlet hath its mirror, and every wind hies to kiss its surface." A man who writes like that has no right to complain if people don't take his goldfish seriously.

That same year I saw Luis Marden's article on Nicaragua in the *National Geographic,* and admired the gaudy red back-half of the 700-pound sawfish in one of his illustrations, but it never occurred to me that there might be some connection between this red sawfish and Stout's goldfish. Probably there isn't any. A few months later, however, Louis Williams, a colleague of mine at Escuela Agrícola Panamericana, brought me fifteen pickled cichlids that he had bought in the market in Managua, and these were something to marvel at.

I had collected cichlids in Mexico and in Honduras and thought I was pretty familiar with the breed, but I had never seen anything like this curious lot. A few were reasonable-looking, dark-barred fish with nothing extraordinary about them, but four were red as a Pensacola snapper, and others, including one of the red ones, had huge, swollen foreheads — high frontal precipices that rose abruptly from ridiculous, piglike snouts for an inch or more before leveling off into the back. To make it worse, neither the butt-headedness nor the red color seemed the mark of a separate species of fish. There appeared to be three species in the lot; one had both red and black representatives and one only red ones, and one of the latter was butt-headed. The third species had butt-headed individuals but no red ones. It was a sorry mess.

At the earliest opportunity I went over to Managua and headed straight for the market. I easily smelled out the fish stalls over in a corner behind a huge heap of armadillos roasted in their shells, and I saw what had caught Williams' eye. There were tray after tray of lake cichlids, in a confusion of kinds and sizes; and scattered among the hundreds, glowing in the gloom of the market, there was the astonishing red-gold of the erythristic variants. Here and there a fishwife had segregated her red fishes in a tray apart, clearly from aesthetic motives rather than taxonomic. Elsewhere the red ones were mixed with the plain; and throughout the whole display — visiting itself without bias upon *guapote*, congo, *machaca*, and mojarra alike, there was the freakish head hump that made each bearer look like its own version of a dolphin.

I got quite excited and talked with the women a long time trying to get their ideas on the meaning of the odd variations. But they were only a little less confused than I was. The two things the people in the market agreed upon were that one mojarra was always red and that one *guapote* was never either red or butt-headed, but for the rest anything went.

The *guapotes* — two species of them — are the biggest

members of the family in the lakes, both reaching a weight
of several pounds. I had been living so close to *guapotes*
in Honduras that I was unwilling to believe the fat old
girl who told me that one of the local *guapotes* sometimes
showed the two variations, and she could find no specimen
to prove it.

The next morning at daylight I stood on the lake shore
before the Barrio de los Pescadores when the fishing boats
came in. The fat fishwife was there too, and as each dugout grated to a stop in the shallows she sloshed out and
peered over the gunwale at the catch on the bottom. Finally, a boat slid in with an uncommonly big chunk of
gold in its flapping freight, and the woman yelled, *¡Ahi,
ve! ¡Ahi 'sta!* and thrashed out to the side of the boat,
clawed about in its cargo, and seized a *guapote* big
enough to bake and the color of *guañín* gold.

The solemn boatman seemed depressed at the eccentric
fervor of his shorecoming welcome and looked at me mis-
trustfully, sure that there was gringo *sonbichismo* somewhere back of the fishwife's behavior. I hastened to reas-
sure him by saying heartily that this was just the kind of
fish I'd been looking for all over the market and all along
the beach. "What kind of fish is it, anyway?" I said.

The fisherman looked relieved. He was back on safe
ground, and his face filled with quiet pride:

"That is the king of the *guapotes*," he said.

I wish I could tell of cleverly devised researches seeking
and finding answers to the problems these curious fishes
present — how many species really show the variations
and how many do not and in what proportions of an affected population each of the conditions occurs; whether

the red color is red pigment or a surface reflection; whether the color and the hump are hereditary, and if so whether inherited as a simple, single-gene character or by some more complex gene system; and whether there may be some factor in the lake environment that either induces the characters directly in the individual fishes or molds red and butt-headed strains by placing selective value on innate capacities for variation.

But as I do with most things, I let the problem slide and got no further than looking up the literature on the lake to see if anyone else had suggested a solution. Tate Regan, author of a monograph on the cichlids and of the fish section in *Biología centrali-americana* showed no excitement over the matter; but Seth Meek, who wrote the only existing account of the fishes of the Nicaraguan lakes, made these remarks: "One of the peculiar ichthic features of the lake is the red, or partially red Cichlids or Mojarras. They are very abundant in the large lakes, and are reported to occur in some of the smaller ones. In Lake Tiscapa [a crater lake near Granada] there are no red forms, nor any red on any of the fishes taken there. Red forms occur in Lakes Asososco, Masaya and Apoyo. I did not find any red fishes in Lagoon Jenicero, and the fishermen there informed me that none were found in it. The cause of this rubrism is not known. I have never seen it in any other body of water. . . . About eight percent of the fishes noticed in the markets of Managua were red, or partially so, and were sold as Mojarras Coloradas. These red forms appear to be the best sellers, but for this I could learn no reason."

So the problem is still waiting, along with a hundred

others, for the lucky student who will someday surely go down and work it out. The red fishes are still there, swimming in the Sweet Sea, like fish images carved from copper-tainted gold — like trinkets the hidalgos took from old Nicaro, bartered for a hawk bell and a lie. They still run like sunbeams before the dugouts, as they fled the bows of the brigantines and frigates standing out across the lake to shoot the white water and thread the forests down to the northern sea, and flock with the *flota* home to Spain.

PART FOUR

Halls of the Mountain Cow

Timber Cruise

NOT long ago I spent a month in the jungle. It was an elegant jungle, real *montaña*, as they say in Central America, and one of the more trackless and undisturbed parts of the great Atlantic Rain Forest that borders the shores from Mexico to Brazil. It was a jungle full of tapirs, which the creoles perversely call "mountain cows," and these are to me the prime requisite of first-class *montaña*.

I had always wanted to get acquainted with the rain forest from the inside, and when Paul Shank, master forester of the United Fruit Company, asked me to go with him on a timber cruise in the wild country back of Pearl Lagoon on the Caribbean side of Nicaragua, no invitation could have pleased me more.

Paul and I were both on the staff of Escuela Agrícola Panamericana in the mountains of south-central Honduras, where we lived next door to each other. While I had been doing a lot of faunal exploration at the time, my jaunts were largely turns about the dry interior uplands on horseback or by truck, but Paul was constantly being called away from pedagogy to appraise distant and exciting terrain — usually down in the howling tropics of the coastal lowlands. When eventually one of his trips coincided in time with my vacation period, Paul could hardly, in humanity, have failed to suggest that I go with him.

Paul not only invited me to go along but had the foresight to assign me a function. His timber cruises are complex affairs which to operate smoothly must exploit the pooled talents of a polyglot personnel, and Paul has found from experience that they go more tranquilly if firearms are kept at a minimum. Thus, he suggested that I sign on as the one expedition meat-hunter to help keep up morale by relieving with game the monotony of constant *gallo pinto* (red-beans-and-rice cooked together) — the standard trail ration of all who travel light in the *montaña*. I took the job, and as it turned out none could have been more to my liking, for it kept me out in front of the cruising parties where I was all alone in the still forest and could skulk along over a hundred miles and more of new-cut trails and soak up sights and sounds and smells.

I kept a journal on the pages of a little blue notebook, now permanently warped from a month in my hip pocket and fat from many wettings. The scribbled pages, recording the strange beasts we met, the meals we ate, and the odd minutiae that make the lives of people who bury themselves in the jungle, seem to me diverting reading, and I have copied them, adding necessary explanation, and — where potent memory demanded — inserting a bit of description but mostly just completing sentences.

MARCH 31. On the 29th we flew down from Tegucigalpa to Managua, and yesterday took a local plane over to the sleepy little Nicaraguan port of Bluefields. The town was named after a Dutch pirate of the seventeenth century called Abraham Bleeveldt who retired and lived with the Indians near here. It was at one time capital of the preposterous little state of Mosquitia which England set up, first as a foil against Spain and a refuge for the buccaneers (who during the late sixteen hundreds made their headquarters at Cabo Gracias a Dios), and later revived as a monarchy with a dynasty of kings amenable to British control of projected canal and railroad routes across Nicaragua by way of the San Juan River basin. The last Mosquito King was retired to Jamaica in 1860, when England ceded part of the territory to Honduras and part to Nicaragua. The Nicaraguan share of the kingdom was held for some time as a reservation before being finally incorporated into the republic as the Department of Zelaya.

The Mosquito people still feel keen nostalgia for their century-old heyday and still hold England in most extraordinary reverence. They are dark folk in whom a hereditary background of Mosquito and Sumo Indian, diluted by the genes of buccaneers and British traders, is to the eye almost completely hidden by African blood, the first injection of which occurred in 1641 when a slave ship was wrecked at the Cape and two hundred Negroes were released. They are poor, pleasant people who call themselves creoles if they are black and Indians if brown, speak English with an astonishing accent, and live in a state of strained mutual tolerance with the Latin minority.

The town looks as the Yamacraw district of Savannah did when I was a boy. Most of the houses are of unpainted wood, with shingles of split *laurel* and wide verandas, all with a silvery patina imparted by time and sun and blown sea-salt. There is no Spanish atmosphere about the place at all except in the commercial district, where the smaller shops are run mostly by mestizos. The big general stores are operated altogether by Chinese, and since our arrival we have spent much of our time in them, going over lists of supplies and searching the jumbled stocks for last-minute additions to our equipment.

The expedition is to leave here tomorrow morning in two sections: one, to include Paul and me, by the inland route on the little launch *Macantaca,* and the other by sea in the company tug *Siquia.* We are scheduled to meet tomorrow evening in Pearl Lagoon, some forty miles to the northward, to complete the organization of the bush party. Río Huahuashan (or Wawashan), which will serve as our highway into the back country, empties into Pearl Lagoon, and Paul is going to hire a *marina* of Lagoon boys, who are superb boatmen, to help with the paddling and portaging. Late this afternoon, I sat in the shade beside the main street of Bluefields, nursing the first can of cold beer that I have seen in months, and watched the life-stream of the town slowly quicken after midday estivation. As if prearranged by a chamber of commerce there was a sudden blaze of local color that tempted me to set the beer can permanently aside. A clop-clop of hooves drew my gaze down the street, where it fell upon a sprightly gray ox, evidently of mixed Brahman and *criollo* blood, approaching at a lively clip. As it trotted past, I noted that its feet bore iron shoes and that it was saddled with a Costa Rican *albarda* in which there sat a black, uniformed messenger holding a dispatch bag. Stirred by this vision I have this evening gone to considerable effort to learn something of its background, but to my frustration have found no one who will even admit that there is anything exciting about a man riding an ox.

APRIL 1. We left Bluefields on the *Macantaca* at 8:00 A.M. and after stopping briefly at the company shops on Schooner Key near the mouth of the Escondido River to take on gas, we entered the maze of mangrove-bordered creeks and estuaries that makes a tortuous connection between Bluefields Lagoon and Pearl Lagoon. As we chugged along in the little old launch, the waterway gradually grew narrower and the mangroves closed in, the climbing sun bore down on us and for a while it was intensely hot. When it seemed that the encroaching mangrove walls were bound to block the channel, we suddenly emerged from the swamp into a canal which someone cut long ago to complete the route. This shallow ditch traverses a wet savanna set with scattered little islands (we call them hammocks back in Florida) of Caribbean pine and skinny, broad-leaved palms, producing a landscape strongly reminiscent of the Florida Everglades. This savanna appears to represent the last southward stand of the widespread Caribbean pine. Although perhaps pure coincidence, it is nevertheless a striking fact that this terminus in pine distribution corresponds almost exactly in latitude with the southernmost extension of the range of two other pines that come down through Honduras and cover the dry mountainsides and cloud-swept ridges of the interior as far south as central Nicaragua, and there suddenly stop completely.

Shortly after noon we entered the little sea called locally by the English name, Pearl Lagoon, and at 3:00 P.M. we met the tug in the channel a half mile off the town of Pearl Lagoon, which for some reason is known more generally as Laguna de Perlas, or merely as Perla. We anchored for the night and took a *cayuca* to shore to have a look at the town, which is the largest of several Mosquito villages scattered about the Lagoon shore. It sprawls over a low, broad, grassy hill that rises from the beach and gives way behind to the seemingly endless savanna. The houses, like those of Bluefields, are mostly of weatherboarding, with split-wood shingles and high, teetery foundation piling. They are shaded by tall *coco*-palms, breadfruit, and enormous, wind-pruned mango trees, which rise from recumbent trunk sections, owing, we were told, to their having made the best of things after a hurricane laid them low in 1912.

The people are creoles who normally communicate in English and Mosquito, but who speak Spanish when they have to. Like Bluefields, the town was for a time capital of the Mosquito Kingdom, and before that well known to the buccaneers who came here to provision their ships and to raise general hell. Its three stores are run by Chinese and appear to constitute the penultimate stage in the commercial evolution of Mosquito Coast Chinese merchants, all of whom dream of ultimate graduation to Bluefields. Paul went into one of the stores to buy more rice and beans for the trip upriver, and I joined a crowd gathered about the veranda to admire the corpse of a fine tom jaguar that had been killed on the edge of town the night before after an intemperate career of pig stealing. The people appeared delighted to see us and opened for us endless green coconuts, the jelly-like contents of which rank among the finer things of life. At dark we paddled out to the tug, where we went to bed after a couple of hours of pleasant but unproductive fishing in the moonlight.

APRIL 2. We awoke at daybreak, had breakfast, which our cook, the gangling but gifted creole Arnold, prepared and served in the little galley of the tug, and after a good deal of yelling and confused trilingual intercourse with shore, we lifted anchors at 7:00 A.M. and crossed the lagoon, reaching the mouth of our river, the Huahuashan, at nine-fifteen. We made a curious train with the tug towing the launch and a string of six slim *cayucas*, all crawling with men and boys of every shade from white to deep ebony. There are thirty-odd people in the party, comprising three functional groups as follows: the *marina*, responsible for *cayuca* transportation, all Mosquitoes recruited from Pearl Lagoon and commanded by Perla's principal citizen, Captain Hebbard, an amiable old master of *cayuca* seamanship; the machete men who open the cruising trails, mostly mestizos, under Robert Henningham, an enormous, deep black, humorous, and highly intelligent former sergeant on the Kingston, Jamaica, police force; and the *cargadores*, who will set up camps and move equipment after we have left the river and who are nearly all old *huleros* (rubber cutters) selected and

143

led by Ernesto Alfaro, white citizen of Bluefields, former colonel in the Nicaraguan army, and probably more intimately acquainted with the Mosquito Coast bush than any other white man alive. The machete crew has just returned from a preliminary trail-cutting expedition up the river and accompanies us now to complete the gridwork of *picadas* which are needed for a systematic sampling of the timber.

During the first two hours after entering the broad, marsh-bordered mouth of the river, we passed hundreds of big tarpon rolling in the channel. As the water freshened, the marshy shore gradually gave way to a palm fringe and vine tangle with dense, low forest behind. At 1:00 P.M. we arrived at the last farm on the river, which is also the last human habitation we shall see for a month. It is the cane plantation of a "Spoñamon" [the black Indians refer to the mestizos and inland Indians as "Spoñamons" (that is, *España* Mans), "Sponish Mons," or merely "Sponiards"] named Vasquez, who settled here with his family several years ago to escape the consequences of certain acts of violence on the Río Cama. The farm is the head of navigation for the tug, which leaves us here and returns to Bluefields. Despite a reputation as a tough *gallo,* Vasquez seems a long-suffering, mild little fellow, and is apparently unruffled at our intrusion, even though we have taken complete charge of the premises, stringing hammocks from every post and projection of his house and setting up our three separate messes in his kitchen and syrup shed. The Mosquito boys swarmed into the nearest cane patch as we landed and are still chewing steadily as they wait for supper.

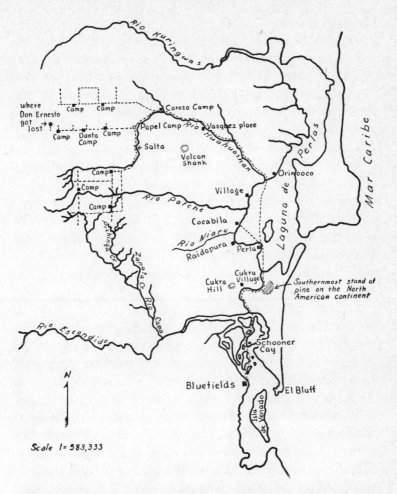

Scale 1 = 583,333

APRIL 3. Last night was our first in the new jungle hammocks, which I had never tried before. They are a combination of bed, roof, and mosquito bar, and an altogether effective invention. I awoke at sunrise, goaded into

145

slow consciousness by the odor of coffee and by the keen, sweet jungle smell that came rolling down with the white river fog. I unzipped my mosquito net and peered out over the cane patch, invisible under a sea of thin mist that lapped the trunk of a huge tree on the far side of the clearing. It was a great, white-boled *palo de agua* which rose dimly a hundred and fifty feet in the semi-opaque air, and from one of its smooth, slender limbs there hung a *panal*, or wasp nest, a flattened cone big as a bushel basket, and almost surely crammed with a rare and irresistible confection of oddly crystallized wasp honey. I had sampled this *dulce de avispa* in Honduras and really regretted that there would not be time to rob the nest. But Arnold was calling me to breakfast and I had to leave the *panal* hanging there in the mist with only grubs to enjoy its hoard.

After breakfast and an effusive parting with Vasquez we left the landing at 6:15 A.M. and headed upriver, the *Macantaca* towing the *cayuca*-train which strung out for fifty yards behind. At 7:30 A.M. we reached a jumbled dam of flood-piled timber and were abruptly deprived of the luxury of the launch, which left us to return to Bluefields after agreeing to rendezvous at this place on April 28. From now on we paddle, pole, haul, and walk. The stream banks have become towering walls of solid green. There is still a little tide in the river but the water is much less turbid. An occasional tarpon still flashes its burnished side in the sunlight; a petty shower sweeps by occasionally, and little bands of predatory needlefish cruise about on the rain-dimpled surface of the water. A freshwater fish fauna also is beginning to show up. We snatch

146

occasional glimpses of copper-and-black *guapotes,* the bass-like cichlids which probably occur in every river in Central America; and from the sandy shallows where the water is rapid our approach routs schools of a flat panfish, also of the cichlid family, which flip and chunk away in frenzied amphibious flight as we approach. For some reason we have seen no turtles, but on three occasions caimans slid sulkily into the water as we neared the mud bars on which they were sunning. At two in the afternoon we made camp on a bluff that has come to be known to river travellers as Corozo because of a single corozo palm that rises on the site.

The Green Tunnel

APRIL 4. We had breakfast by lantern light, and in the gray beginning of dawn pushed on upriver. Shallows and rapids are more numerous now, and we move mostly by poling. A couple of hours above Corozo camp we passed a sand bar, the smooth surface of which was ploughed with fresh caiman trails. On seeing these the Mosquito boys howled with delight, jumped overboard, splashed through the shallow water to the sand bar, and began to dig furiously. Within a matter of seconds they had uncovered a cache of thirty-one caiman eggs, and in a nearly confluent cavity they found the nest of an iguana containing forty-one eggs. Whether this juxtaposition came about through chance or through design we could not decide. The caiman had laid first, the eggs of the iguana having been placed at a higher level than the other nest and nearly over it. Maybe it was opportunism that led the gravid iguana, reconnoitering the bar

148

for suitable incubating sand, to choose for her own pur-
poses the mound of newly tilled sand that covered the
eggs of the caiman. We even toyed with the irresponsible
conceit that it was the power of suggestion — that the
nesting rites of the caiman were witnessed by the iguana
from her basking limb above the bar, where she felt her
own hormones stir in sympathy to give a new consciousness of the bulge of her half-peck of leathery eggs. Most
probably it was just coincidence. The Mosquito boys gave
this matter no thought at all, but divided up the eggs and
either sucked them forthwith or hid them among their
belongings. Paul, Alfaro, and I continued to discuss the
problem at length, however, reclining in state on the
canvas-covered cargo as the *cayucas* moved on slowly up
the river. When the subject had been exhausted, the talk
turned to tapirs, directed thither by the increasingly numerous go-down tapir trails along the banks of the river.
Ernesto said without turning a hair that he has seen tame
tapirs used as beasts of burden by *huleros*. He claims that
they do well in this service, except for a tendency to
plunge into any body of water they encounter and to
walk across it on the bottom, to the detriment of whatever soluble cargo they may be carrying. We passed a
black-and-white anteater in a bamboo tree on the bank,
and somewhat later a *pisote* (coati), which I shot at the
insistence of the boat boys who wanted to eat it. We made
camp for the night on a low bluff which the river-wise of
our gang agree is called Papel (paper), although why,
when, or by whom it was so named none can say. For
supper Arnold made an omelet of caiman eggs which, with
the last of a ham we had brought, made good victualing.

149

APRIL 5. It rained hard last night, but our jungle hammocks made night rains more a diversion than a annoyance they might be under other circumstances. After a breakfast of fricasseed *pisote*, Paul, Henningham, and I struck out through the woods on a five-kilometer hike that intercepted the boats where they were stopped by a series of superb waterfalls far upstream. The falls are in two groups separated by a deep blue pool, perhaps two hundred yards across and alive with striking fish, most of which are *guapotes*. We had to wait here for two hours before the last of the boats arrived, and I passed the time alternately cursing my lack of fishing tackle and stalking curassows, of which I shot a handsome cock as big as a turkey gobbler. I found on the *vega* a caecilian — a legless, eyeless, burrowing amphibian, representing an extraordinary order of vertebrate animals that I had known before only from textbooks.

When all the boats had come up, the entire mob fell to and hauled the heavy *cayucas* over, around, or through the falls and rapids, a job that cost us two more hours and prodigious amounts of talk. We made camp at noon, a short distance above the upper falls and in an altogether enchanting spot. For lunch Arnold regaled us with a female iguana stewed with her eggs, a dish held in high reverence locally, and not unjustly so. Iguanas are so sought after that even this far up the river they seem much less abundant than they should be. We have caught only three of them, and while we have seen others high in the trees above the river, these have been mostly old five- and six-foot males. The males are tough and not nearly so succulent as the pregnant females, which at this season are apparently too heavy with eggs to climb freely and are usually found on low limbs or even on the ground. Although an arboreal lizard, the iguana is in my experience wholly limited to the vicinity of water, into which it dives from the most astonishing heights when approached. On several occasions I have stood quietly watching five or six iguanas browsing on *guanacaste* leaves on limbs fully fifty feet above the water, and then have stepped suddenly into the open to flush them from their high perches and admire the casual way they took the long drop and smashing contact with the water below. Once in the river an iguana seems to be no less at home than an alligator. In some of the clear tributaries of the Huahuashan we have watched the behavior of iguanas under water, where they fold their legs back and swim easily and swiftly with the primitive undulations used by most aquatic vertebrates when in a hurry. They usually go directly to the bottom and nose about until a crevice or log jam has been found; and in this take refuge, remaining sometimes as long as half an hour. When thus submerged iguanas are easily approached and caught by a diver. It is thus that the Lagoon boys usually catch them, although like other Caribbean people they nearly always whistle a tune to an iguana sighted on the bank, in the firm belief that this charms the creature into passivity. Whether or not the music contributes anything, I have never seen anyone but these whistling Mosquitoes catch an iguana on the ground.

This is as far as the boats will take us. Tomorrow we head into the *montaña* on foot with ten boys to cut trail and carry equipment. The rest of the people will remain

on the *vega* with the boats and heavy gear to await our
return. I can't help envying the boys we are leaving behind. This is easily the most fetching camp site I have
ever seen. The crystal-clear river invades the woods here
and there in racing distributaries that have been ravelled
out of the main stream by some local disruption of the
gradient, and these surround little stage-set islands, each
with a big tree or two rising from a heavy carpet of
maidenhair fern. The water sparkles in splotched sunlight under the tall *vega* timber, and long reaches beat
themselves into white froth among huge rhyolite boulders
or hiss fast over table-smooth ledges, to plunge with a
sustained roar into broad, deep pools so clear that schools
of cichlids and giant shrimps can be seen moving across
the bottom. Only the thought of the things to be missed
out in the high rain forest beyond the *vega* reconciles me
to leaving this lovely spot.

Madre Selva

*A*PRIL 6.   This morning we got up at four o'clock to
prepare to pack out into the forest. After a quick breakfast
the bush crew went into action with a fast, quiet efficiency
that to me was altogether unexpected. They disappeared
briefly into the darkness to return with armfuls of six-foot
lengths of the inner bark of three kinds of trees that grow
hereabouts. With these strips, which are as strong as rawhide, each of the *cargadores* trussed up a 100-pound pack
with sump line and shoulder harness, tried and adjusted
it for fit, and then stood waiting for the rest of the cruising
party to move out into the faint trail that would take us
away from the river and into the timber block.

Meanwhile, Joe, one of the Perla boys, had gone into
the woods in search of what he called a "mon-wit." This
turned out to be a fifty-foot length of a liana so flexible
and tough that it would not break when overhand knots
were pulled tight along its length. This cord was to be

used as a surveyor's chain to measure distances along the cruising routes. I asked about the name "mon-wit" and was told that the vine was so called because, though strong enough to be useful cordage, a single "mon" could nevertheless haul it down from the trees. That left the "wit," and I claim some credit for recognizing in it the good English word *withe*, which, though dormant in my vocabulary, was probably an everyday word to the pirates who founded Joe's English. Almost the entire expedition gathered around to talk about wits and to assure me that there were two other classes of them — one known generically as "wooman-wits," that a man could send his wife after, and another called "ox-wits" because they could only be dragged down by a team of oxen. These latter are widely used as bindings for ox-yokes, not only in Nicaragua, but in Honduras as well. They probably have at least the tensile strength of quarter-inch Manila rope.

It would be hard to find a more diverse group than this amalgamation of Henningham's machetemen and Alfaro's *cargadores*. They range from deep black to white through every possible intermediate shade, and misuse three languages with reckless indiscrimination. All, however, are superb woodsmen. Their woodcraft is more than a useful accomplishment — it is a way of staying alive, and hardly one of them but would at one time or another have died in the woods had his skill been defective. Most of them are old *huleros*. To such people there is no ordeal in a ten-mile walk with a 100-pound load, even though the way be through rain and mud of trackless selva, into and out of bamboo brakes, huiscoyol bogs, and steep-walled ravines, with the end of the trail offering only a wet camp in which to swing a hammock and eat a fistful of *gallo pinto*. This is just a day's work to these folk — an alternative to fishing or planting a bean patch or going to Bluefields. Walking out in front with no load other than a gun and a haversack, I felt self-conscious, but when I hinted at the inequity, the Indian Sosa pointed out that it was inevitable and proper, since his job would quickly kill me.

As we sloshed along the dark, wet trail, picking out by flashlight the occasional cut stem that marked the route, Sosa told me about Juana Alvarez, the only female rubber cutter in the Mosquitia, who worked the *montaña* up the Río Cama during the last war when rubber prices were high. She operated alone, in an area six days' journey from the nearest house. Through five years, each with a ten-month rainy season, and no dry season at all, her home was a narrow palm shelter under which she hung her hammock and rubber dufflesack over the endless mud. Like all of her calling, she toiled from sun-up until ten at night coaxing the precious milk from one lone *hule* after another (after having originally located the isolated and scattered trees through some mystic sense wholly incomprehensible to a North American), packing the latex to camp, and cooking the simple rations for the next day's rounds. The day of the *hulero* (and of the *hulera*) is done till another war; Juana now lives in a real cabin on Río Cama, and I hope we get a chance to go see her before we leave the coast.

This evening an *oso caballo* (a giant anteater, known to Costa Rican legend as *dueño del monte*, or master of the bush) passed by, calling in the jungle. At least that's what everybody swears it was. We first heard the arresting

155

lament far in the northeast, seemingly miles away. It slowly came nearer until it was only a few hundred yards out from the dim circle of our firelight, and then moved off toward the south to die away at last in some far barranca. The cry comprised three or four strange, sad, musical notes, descending the scale and repeated at frequent but irregular intervals. *OO-oo-oo-oo*, it went, the notes falling in slow elision and combining a disturbingly human quality with the reedy suggestion of some little-used stop of a pipe organ. It was the most stirring animal voice I had ever heard. It had an eerily lovely, and yet somehow distressing, quality which affected even the *macheteros* and moved them to pause in their perennial noisy fireside discussion of women. I don't see how the *oso caballo*, with his long tubular snout, could possibly have been the source of these sounds, but there's no arguing with the unanimous opinion of the *montañeros*.

APRIL 7.   Again it rained during the night but, zipped up in our cocoon-like jungle hammocks, we stayed dry and snug. Some of the boys who had skimped on their palm-leaf shelters got wet, but they seemed not to mind much. A tapir came into camp just after midnight and prowled about, leaving tracks everywhere among the sleepers. Arnold says he heard the noise but thought it was I returning from one of my night-collecting forays, and so did not sound an alarm. This irked me no end, since I would rather see a tapir than anything the forest holds and have not yet come face to face with one. At 5:00 A.M. we set out on the first of the timber cruises for which everything so far has been merely preliminary. Paul was disappointed at the scarcity of big mahogany, although we saw a few fine trees. One good tree per hectare is regarded as a commercially workable stand of mahogany, and the average here is far lower than that. On a little ridge I jumped a deer and flushed a flock of *pavas* or guans (or as the Mosquitoes say, *cuam*) — loud-voiced gallinaceous birds that look like small, rangy turkeys. A little farther on I saw four curassows, and shot one of them. There were many tapir and tiger signs everywhere, but I had no view of the beasts that left them. We had several showers during the morning, and the ravine walls were sloppy and a nuisance to climb.

There is a little bird here that keeps my nerves on edge by making a noise exactly like the snapping of a twig under a heavy foot. After prowling along the trail with all the stealth I can achieve and listening intently for the eerily elusive creatures of the forest, this sudden snap at close range carries the shock of a pistol shot. The bird is one of the manakins and the male is very handsome, with a deep black body and crimson head. Like other manakins he practices a lurid courtship rite that involves the clearing of all debris from a small area of the forest floor and the performing of aerial acrobatics above this spot, while emitting the curious cracking and popping sounds that obtrude so harshly upon my tense stalking. The Mosquito people call the little bird "pop-match," which is better imagery than they usually attain in their animal names.

APRIL 8.   More thunderstorms last night, but here in the high forest there is little blown rain, and a narrow piece of thatch usually keeps everything directly under it dry. We moved camp ten kilometers farther back today, and in addition cruised nine kilometers of timber *picadas*, travelling the nineteen kilometers between 5:30 A.M. and 1:30 P.M. The mud was deep in the low places and the *hondonada* walls were slippery, but these are small annoyances to balance against the excitement of walking these trails. The routes are cut by compass bearing and take the jungle as it comes, compromising with no foible of the terrain — digressing for neither swamp nor blowdown *breña* nor bamboo brake. They thus afford a true and otherwise unattainable picture of the virgin rain forest in all its aspects. To walk such lanes through the towering *selva* is pure delight, and no naturalist could ask a higher privilege.

Today I walked a hundred yards to half a mile ahead of the timber counters. The *picadas* were easy to follow except in the occasional cathedral-like climax groves in which huge *almendro, cedro macho,* and monkey-pot trees shut out all direct light a hundred feet and more above a clean understory in which there was not even enough underbrush to furnish stems to cut as trail markers. Frogs were numerous, and twice I found myself amid swarms of incredibly gaudy little ground-dwelling hylids, colored a glowing ruby above and vivid turquoise on the sides and belly. I saw four curassows and heard several others. The call is like a single note on a bass viol; or even more like the "voom" of a "bull roarer," the flat stick that children tie by one end to a cord and twirl about their heads to make a fine, deep roaring sound. I shot one curassow for supper, and for variety added to it an agouti, a big rodent, known locally as *guatuso*, that runs off squealing in panic when disturbed along the trail. Two pair of motmots, of a species larger, less delicately colored, and of stronger voice than the highland form that I know, sat on limbs and watched me as I slid and clawed into and out of their ravines, and hooted incessantly in a deep, strident monotone. The motmots are a tropical family of extroverted birds that specialize in fancy shades of blue and often have some of the tail feathers bare-shafted back to a ridiculous little terminal plume. For a long time ornithologists have browbeaten each other over the question of the origin of the bare shafts — whether they are stripped by the birds themselves or are inherited — and while I have the feeling that Alexander Skutch has recently settled the dispute, I can't remember how.

We have left the Huahuashan drainage temporarily behind, and our present camp is on the bank of a little tributary of Río Pichinga, which in turn flows into Río Cama of the Escondido system. I was tired after today's hike, and it was a great luxury to bathe in the cold creek and lie in my hammock in the cool, green afternoon, watching the boys putting up their leaf *casitas* and Arnold cooking supper. Except for the frequent rains the rain-forest weather is perfect — far more pleasant than that outside along the coast. Midday temperatures have ranged between seventy-eight and eighty-one degrees Fahrenheit, and we always use a blanket at night. Since we got into the deep woods there have been no mosquitoes at all and only a few ticks. After three years of rambling in the mountains of Honduras, this rain-forest expedition seems idyllic and almost wholly devoid of hardship.

APRIL 9. Last night I was up until midnight walking the creek bed in unsuccessful search of tapirs. The creek makes an ideal trail for night collecting and headlight hunting. Not only does it attract animals but one snaps no dry twigs in the water, and the possibility of getting lost is almost nonexistent if one only keeps account of the order and relations of the tributary streams passed. I collected four species of frogs and caught several big freshwater crabs and half a dozen magnificent *camarones* — the succulent lobster-like shrimps that inhabit most of the rocky streams of this region. I boiled the crabs and shrimps on my return to camp, and although Paul and Alfaro moaned and grumbled over the racket I made, they bore no grudge after Arnold served us shrimps and crab meat on johnny-cake toast for breakfast. We walked only five kilometers today, cutting the cruise short when a blinding rainstorm came up in the late morning. On the trail I collected two snakes, one of them a little horned viper on a palm leaf. This was the only poisonous snake that we have encountered to date. When we reached camp with a couple of hours to spare, Paul helped me drag a little seine in the creek, which is alive with *guapotes*, eels, catfish, and shoals of silvery characins. Most of the streams in this section are bamboo-bordered, with palm jungle back of the marginal brakes, and the higher ground and well-drained ridges covered by open stands of big timber. Since this latter is certainly virgin as far as post-Columbian man is concerned, we were amazed to find great tracts of it curiously youthful in appearance, and almost certainly not primeval forest. Paul believes that these areas may have grown up after destruction of pre-existing woods by a hurricane that ripped through here at some time in the relatively recent past.

Where huge trees have fallen within the past year or so, taking with them their weaker near neighbors, the new spot of light has been exploited by a tangled host of sprawling, snaking vines and creepers that canopy the clearing as if a vast green circus tent had collapsed over it. Through such blowdowns our trails become tunnels.

I suddenly realized today that the language of the expedition has changed. Out on the river it was predominately English, with the *marina* lapsing into terse Mosquito when emergency threatened, or when any aspect of the handling of the *cayucas* was discussed. Back here in the bush the *cargadores* and *macheteros* have become the dominant group; and since they are all mestizos, we talk only Spanish.

APRIL 10. This was an exciting day. To begin with, a mountain cow, waiting till my midnight fire died down, walked by in the swirling mist of the creek bed, not twenty feet from where my hammock hung. Its splashing awoke me, but before I could put on my wet shoes it took to the ferns and I never saw it. Just before dawn a steady drizzle began to fall, and as we prepared to depart this became a heavy rain. Only a few minutes out from camp I shot a *pava*, a *guatuso*, three of the immense forest quail that bellow in stentorian and utterly unquaillike voice just after dark and just before day, and a brocket — a goatlike little red forest deer with huge eyes and simple spike antlers. That this clearly was all the meat we needed reinforces the shame of the following event.

I believe I have conveyed something of my desire, amounting by now to an obsession, to see a tapir in the woods. With respect to my attitude toward varmints, I have always been afflicted with a Dr.-Jekyll-and-Mr.-Hyde complex — an altogether unresolved conflict between the instincts of a naturalist and the urge to shoot things. These dual drives have given me a lot of trouble from time to time, and today they did their worst. This morning in the rain I finally came upon a mountain cow that did not see, smell, or hear me first. The ponderous beast lay half sunk in a pool in the vinegrown floodplain of a little creek. I looked down on him from a curve in the trail that skirted a steep undercut bank. I could have stood who knows how long savoring the fulfillment of my desire to see a tapir, watching this one in his most private moments as he rolled and snorted and steamed himself in his oxbow bathtub; but I muffed the chance. Through inexorable reflex I raised my puny rifle and started shooting as fast as I could pull the trigger. I don't suppose the stream of hollow-point bullets that rattled slantwise against his flinty thorax did the tapir any harm; I hope not. But they put him in a great sweat to get out of the water and away from the neighborhood. He floundered out of the mudhole with most incongruous agility. Ignoring in his haste the usual exit, he burst easily through the solid palisade of lianas and vine-strung saplings that enclosed his retreat. Heading straight for a bamboo thicket, he again sought no trail, but drove squarely into the dense stand of fishing poles, bending the live canes and snapping the dead ones that opposed him with the racket of a dozen rifles. He charged away through the brake with unabating fury, and

I stood and listened in complete dejection as the noise of the popping canes grew feeble with distance.

APRIL 11. We were up at four-thirty this morning. The pain of arising in the predawn was relieved considerably when Arnold broiled the three quail for Paul, Ernesto, and me. These elegant birds are just as good to eat as northern bobwhites and are three or four times as big. We were off on our tour just before six o'clock, and almost at once I shot a tinamou, known to the local *gente*, and in Honduras too, for that matter, as *gongalola*. There are two common species here, one as big as a good-sized hen and the other much smaller. Tinamous are a strange, primitive family of birds most closely related to the ostriches. They have no tails. They have singularly lovely voices and flesh of ghastly greenish transparency, becoming unrelieved white on being cooked, but nevertheless fairly good to eat if not dried out in preparation. Tinamous have an annoying habit of crouching in concealment beside the trail until one almost steps on them, and at the last moment losing their nerve and flushing in an explosive roar of wingwork that is shocking in its abrupt violence. Farther along the trail I surprised a band of white-faced monkeys in a clump of *bratarra* bamboos. What they hoped to find there that might warrant their risking evisceration by the hellish spines that arm *bratarra*, I cannot imagine. Having no high retreat to retire to when I appeared below, they worked themselves into a frenzy of resentment. Many of the females had young, which they clutched with pitiful anxiety, and the males all behaved with impressive virility, barking, urinating, throwing down twigs and trash, and even springing halfway down a cane-stem to grimace at point-blank range and with awful malice. We made camp at 1:00 P.M., and I took a swim, washed some clothes, and rested in my hammock. In this muddy ravine terrain we seem to like to walk no more than seven hours a day. Today's camp is the most attractive we have had since leaving the river, being located on the bank of a clear stream with a waterfall that tumbles into a blue pool some forty feet in diameter and deep enough to make a fine swimming hole. We are in a palm jungle here. The dominant tree in the dense woods is a tall, slim palm with numerous proproots dropping from the stem for a distance of two or three feet above the ground. Our elevation is one hundred fifty feet. At 2:00 P.M. the temperature of the air was eighty-two degrees Fahrenheit and that of the creek water seventy-two degrees Fahrenheit.

APRIL 12.   Two men are sick today, one with a fever of unknown cause, and one with an ugly carbuncle on the calf of his leg. Alfaro doped the former with quinine, and into the latter we hopefully injected a hundred thousand units of penicillin. There were two hundred extra pounds of *carga* to be divided among the rest of the crew, and for the first time there has been some grumbling. I like these *carga* boys very much, but I should hate to have them angry with me. Mostly they are pretty untrammelled chaps, and at least two are old *sandinistas* who "entertain" Paul and me with tales of their castrating and cutting the heads off United States Marines during the rebellion. While we have had no rain for two days and walking on the level is much easier, in other respects to-day's hike was the roughest to date. When we left this morning, Henningham said the trail would be "some hum-bugged by creeks," and he was right. We climbed and slid all day, travelling as far vertically as overland, and taking eight hours to do a three-hour stretch of trail. I shot a curassow early in the morning and repented the act on every remaining ravine wall, where the dangling ten-pound bird became a real incubus. In a tonka bean (*almendro*) grove I found a congregation of *guatusos*. Hitherto I have seen them only singly, but here they formed what appeared to be a colony; every few yards for a quarter of a mile one of the timorous creatures bounced off among the buttressed trunks, yelping hoarsely and wuffing, and finally diving into the mouth of a burrow.

APRIL 13.   Last night's camp was our last in this block of timber, and we are now back on the river *vega* at our earlier camp site by the waterfalls. Before breaking camp this morning, Alfaro gave Paul and me a lesson in bush medicine. One of the *macheteros* had been complaining of a red swelling under his shoulder blade, and another dis-played a similar lump on the side of his foot. Without hesitation Alfaro diagnosed both cases as *torsola* worms, and to each swelling in turn he applied the lighted end of a cigarette and held it as close as the patient could stand for a minute or so. From each mound there emerged the head end of a small grub, and this Alfaro seized and plucked out between thumb and forefinger. The boy with the carbuncle is much better today, having amazed us by offering to carry a pack.

On the trail out to the river Charlie passed me when I relinquished my customary meat-hunting post at the head of the file to catch frogs in a seep for fifteen minutes or so. When I resumed the trail I immediately began to notice the tracks of a jaguar in the damp places. This was an enormous animal, its footprints being strikingly broader and deeper than any of the numerous others we have seen. After a bit I realized that many of its footprints were superimposed on Charlie's, and that the great gaudy beast was probably even now gliding along the *picada* between Charlie and me. It was, in fact, trailing Charlie; not in an ugly spirit, or with gastronomic implications of any sort, but trailing him from sheer feline caprice. The situation took me back to an afternoon in the Florida scrub when I sat on a deer stand on a low hill overlooking a recent burn and watched two figures move off toward the horizon — one of them an ant-sized deerhunter who believed himself all alone, and the other a trailing bobcat. Now, finding myself the third party in a similar parade, I began to walk as fast as I could in the hope of catching sight of the jaguar, but though the trail continued to within two or three hundred yards of the river-bank camp, I saw no *tigre*. I couldn't have missed it by much, however, since when I arrived Charlie had just unstrapped his *carga* and was sitting on it to blow after his long hike.

The Lagoon boys who stayed here to watch the supply dump we left behind say that a tiger, perhaps the same one that trailed Charlie, came into camp one night while we were away. Shortly after we reached camp it began to rain, and I was glad of the excuse to crawl into my hammock for a nap. When the rain stopped we swam in the river, shaved, and had supper, for which the Lagoon boys, who had fished most of the time we were away, furnished a big baked *guapote*.

APRIL 14. Last night, during a letup in the rain, I went out on the rocks in the rapids with my headlight and fish grains and speared *camarones*. I also got a good-sized *guapote* and one of the big gobies known locally as *dormilones*. It continued to rain until about 3:00 A.M. and began again at six, and Paul and I enjoyed the unfamiliar luxury of staying holed up in our hammocks while Henningham and his durable mob moved on ahead to cut *picadas* in the next block. This must have been a nasty job, for the rain kept up, at times with terrific violence, until afternoon. Just as it stopped we witnessed a classic tropical drama when the camp was invaded by army ants. They came suddenly, in what seemed millions, heralded only by a panic-stricken host of crickets, spiders, roaches, beetles, millipedes, sow bugs, harvestmen, frogs, and lizards. The frenzied hegira of little creatures out in front was more of a trial than the ants themselves to Arnold, who was cooking dinner, since in their dismay they jumped or crawled or fluttered into every open pot and container, and with pathetic eagerness scaled his slender black calves to take sanctuary in trousered darkness. Paul and I zipped up our mosquito bars and watched with interest until it seemed that the meal would be delayed; then we got out a rotenone-DDT duster and an aerosol bomb and literally piled up a peck of arthropods around Arnold's installations.

Just after dark Paul and I and two "Spanish Indians"

took a *cayuca* and went downstream as far as the lower
falls. Here I shot a *tepescuinte*, or paca, a large, solidly
built, longitudinally striped rodent that is more highly
prized for its meat than any other mammal in the *montaña*. When I fired, the *tepescuinte* made one prodigious
vertical leap, appearing to us in the boat as fully five feet
in height, and then fell back into the darkness beyond our
line of vision on the steep eight-foot bank. We moved the
boat up, and I climbed the bank and located the animal
just where we had seen it fall. It seemed completely dead,
but when I felt for a grip on its hind leg the creature
burst into a spasmic series of gargantuan leaps that so
startled me that I lost my balance and toppled off the
bank into the boat, where almost at once the *tepescuinte*
fell after me. There was a flurry of disorder before one of
the boys succeeded in cracking the paca on the back of its
neck with the off-edge of a machete, while the other pulled
me from under a seat, and Paul fished my gun out of the
river. After this we saw a number of crocodiles, one very
large one, but no more game.

APRIL 15.   We are still waiting for Henningham to return from his trail-cutting trip. Everybody seems to welcome the opportunity to stay in the same camp for more
than one night — a real blessing in such a pleasant camp
as this, which, incidentally, has somehow come to be
known as "Santa Ana." After making a pole out of the
dry, light petiole of a palm leaf, I spent the day fishing.
I caught a fine string of *guapotes* and several of a kind of
characin known in many parts of Central America as
sabalo (*Brycon*). These fish are much admired in Hon-

duras by the few flyrod anglers there, who rate them with young tarpon for spirit on a line. For dinner we had the *tepescuinte,* which made this the most momentous meal of the trip. Arnold roasted the plump carcass after scalding and scraping it as he would a young pig, which it much resembles in appearance but excels in flavor. The meat is white but not dry or overdense. It is constantly self-basted while cooking by the exudations of an even layer of fat which covers it, and which fries the skin to succulent cracklings. After two weeks in the woods a meal like this becomes a well-nigh holy event.

APRIL 16. Henningham returned during the night, and this morning we loaded the *cayucas* and sent them downstream to make camp at Papel, where we stopped on our way up. Paul, Charlie, and I made the trip on foot in order to look over a patch of promising forest lying between the two camps, but not included in the original cruise plan. On the way I collected two interesting mud turtles that were copulating in a swamp and a small snake that lay in the trail, and just before reaching Papel, I managed to shoot a fish that I have been trying to get for the collection for some time. It is a handsome cichlid that the Mosquito people call *tuba,* much like an angelfish in general appearance, with lavender ground color, rosy red breast, and a deep black spot at the base of the tail. At Papel we found not only the *cayucas* from upstream but two boatloads of Lagoon boys whom we had sent all the way back to Perla for supplies twelve days ago. These boys are all quite young and high-spirited, and their trip was a hectic one. On the way down they

surprised a tiger on a rock in the river and killed it. A
Perla boy named Joe shot it with the only firearm they
had — a repulsively rusty singleshot twenty-two of a breed
that sold for three dollars and a half when I was a boy.
Joe had six hollow-point cartridges that I had doled out
to him, and he shot them all at the tiger before it slid
into the river dead. They fished it out of the water with
poles, skinned it, and went on in a high state of exultation.
Less than an hour later they drifted by in helpless frustration as another jaguar stood on a bluff and watched
them; and not long after that the canoes drew up across
the mouth of a little steep-walled cove to cut off all
avenue of escape for a huge bull tapir that wallowed
there. The Mosquito people love to eat mountain cow
(even as far toward civilization as Bluefields it fetches
prices topped only by those for *tepescuinte*); and here
in a natural corral was enough meat to feed all Perla and
to make every boy in the two canoes a hero if only they
could deliver it. Their only weapons were sticks, stones,
machetes, and a fish spear, and they battled the poor
tapir with these for a while; finally, however, they saw
that one of them would surely be trampled by the plung-
ing beast before it suffered any damage. As a last des-
perate venture, Joe took a long, sharp butcher knife and
climbed the bank above the tapir, hoping that he might
drop to its back and find a soft spot somewhere before
being thrown. When the others had maneuvered the
mountain cow to a point near the bank, Joe jumped and
skidded off the broad back, landing face down in the
mud. Thus stimulated, the tapir bolted, charged the un-
tended canoes, pushing them aside like corks, and found

asylum in the bosom of the river. The Lagoon people, especially the young folk, talk English in a high-pitched, piping monotone, with each syllable detached like a separate word; and when the boys all started telling of their trip at once, the excited chorus was a wild and almost wholly unintelligible chant.

A band of white-faced monkeys paid us an indignant visit this afternoon. It seems strange that these capuchins, which appear so well adjusted and even eager to please when in the company of an organ grinder, should be so consistently irritable and restless in the wild state. The irascible bands that we meet contrast strongly with the families of easygoing howler monkeys that often sprawl on limbs for hours on end to gaze down with lazy interest at men and their works, and with the parties of spider monkeys, which stage protracted exhibitions of acrobatics apparently only to impress the observer with their breathtaking agility. The river here is deeper and less noisy than at Santa Ana, and it runs over a cobble bed instead of over bedrock and boulders. As consolation for the mountain cow fiasco, which depressed him considerably, I gave Joe three more of my precious hollow-points this afternoon, and he went out and killed a deer. This cheered up all the Lagoon boys. At supper Paul and I eschewed the new venison to polish off the last of the *tepescuinte* — a rotund ham stuck with garlic and warmed over above a smoky fire. It was very comforting. This evening I went up the river to spear fish and got eleven, mostly *guapotes* and *dormilones*. I took my gun along and spotted and was about to shoot a *tepescuinte*, when a tapir took fright above me on the bank and blundered down almost on top of the *tepescuinte,* only to plunge into the water and disappear.

APRIL 17. Last night we were awakened by a terrific clamor across the river. It was the most outrageous din, in fact, that I have heard in these noisy woods. It was nothing to be endured in silence, and I yelled an anxious inquiry to the camp in general.

Mono colorado (spider monkey) was the sleepy diagnosis from several hammocks.

"Well, what in hell ails them?" I went on. *¡Qué les pasa? Carájo!*

Pasa el tigre por abajo (there's a tiger under their tree), came the unanimous pronouncement.

The monkeys continued to yelp and scream in hysterical chorus. Sleep was out of the question, and I spent the time marvelling at the iron nerve of a jaguar that would of its own free will stand so long under the mad bivouac across the river. After what must have been nearly an hour the tiger presumably went away, and the lament tapered off to an occasional shriek of recollected horror, and I dropped off to sleep. We made a fifteen-kilometer cruise today, returning to Papel for the night. This morning I had a good shot at a fine buck deer — not a brocket, but the tropical counterpart of the northern white-tail — but he was running among trees and I missed. Later on I collected what must be one of the largest of all hummingbirds — a gross creature with no hummingbird delicacy and much more like a kingfisher in appearance. Perhaps it is a kingfisher. Although I'm not prepared to collect birds on this trip, I couldn't resist the temptation to make a skin of this one to confound Margie with on my return. On numerous occasions I have shined the eyes of a small, shy animal along the banks of the creeks in which I walk with my headlight nearly ever night. I finally gave up hope of seeing one of the creatures at close hand alive, and shot a specimen. It turned out to be a handsome rat, as big as a fox squirrel and with pelage composed of flat, lance-shaped spines hidden among long, sleek hairs.

APRIL 18.   Last night, as I was wading into the river to light for turtles and spear fish, Charlie yelled at me to stop. He came down to the bank and motioned toward a rock bar upstream where a small group of the oversized toads, commonly and ineptly referred to as "marine toads" (because of the technical name, *Bufo marinus*), were giving voice to their trilling love song. The call is a baritone whistle, not overly obtrusive but with great carrying power, and with the ventriloquistic quality that makes the source of so many frog songs hard to locate. It is a coarsened caricature of the sweet trill of the toads that sing in garden pools in the eastern United States.

Terciopelos, said Charlie, and added in Spanish, "Better not wade in the river tonight."

Terciopelo means "velvet," and is the name usually given to the bushmaster in recognition of the velvety dark markings of that formidable snake; but Charlie applies it to the fer-de-lance (which elsewhere is more often called *barba amarilla*, in reference to the light-yellowish chin characteristic of that species).

"You mean the *bichos* doing the singing?" I asked.

¡Cómo no! said Charlie. *Son terciopelos.*

173

"Oh, no," I corrected him. "Those are toads."

¡La puta! said Charlie. "*Son terciopelos.* I've heard them all my life."

"Did you ever see one singing?" I inquired.

Sosa and two other "Spoñamons" came over to reinforce Charlie.

Son terciopelos, they stated with finality.

A little frantic, I grabbed my headlight and sloshed up the river edge to the bar, walked out to the shallow dead-water flat where the toads had fallen silent at my approach, and seized one of the burly beasts in each hand. I took them back to camp and held them before my opponents.

Miren que son sapos, I exulted.

"Those are toads all right, but what were singing were *terciopelos,*" said Charlie. "These things can't sing."

"Can't sing!" I shrieked. "*¡Ave Maria santísima!* Come out on the bar with me and I'll show you. *No hay que discutirlo más.* Come on out there and be quiet for five minutes and you'll see them singing all around you."

¡A la puta! said Charlie (and the others echoed, *¡La puta!*). "I've been living around here all my life, and I know better than to go fooling around in the river when the *terciopelos* are singing!"

For a time I was saddened by this intrusion of mysticism into the woodsmanship of my new friends and respected mentors. But then I began to realize that this was just another demonstration of the dogged consistency with which non-zoologists everywhere exclude from their woodslore even the most elementary grasp of the natural history of reptiles, and accept any cock-and-bull story concerning them. To illustrate this with an example that shows also striking parallel in details: I know a dozen Florida farmers — intelligent and successful men with deep freezers at home and children in college, who will slow down as they drive past a rain-flooded flatwoods, in which a thousand tiny oak toads cheep, to call your attention to the "scorpions whistling." By "scorpions" they mean lizards of the genus *Eumeces*, and since no one of their set has ever been so shiftless as to slog out in the wet to check the identification, they have no cause to doubt it. And thus, Charlie, who can name every tree along a rain-forest trail, and Sosa, who has laid out and worked rubber lines ten days' walk from human habitation, feel no responsibility for testing the tradition, handed down from who knows what remote origin, that vipers sing on the rocks in the river!

I went on out in the river, without the blessing of the Spanish Indians, and speared a fine mess of *guapotes* and collected a good lot of frogs and two turtles — one of them of the genus *Pseudemys*, in which I have been interested for a long time, and the other of a semiaquatic group (*Geomyda*) widespread in tropical America. This morning we left Papel for Corozo camp down the river, reaching it before noon. We puttered around with our gear this afternoon, and expect to go to bed early in anticipation of another week's tour in the *montaña* beginning tomorrow.

APRIL 19. We quit the river at 5:30 A.M. for another trip into the bush. Shortly after leaving the *vega* we began to get into some of the handsomest forest that we have seen so far. The trees are immense, and on the ridges there is little undergrowth other than a scattering of cane-like palms and soft-stemmed, gloom-loving shrubs and saplings. It is easy to get lost in this sort of woods, since the *picada*, which is one's only link with the outside world, is no more than an occasional blaze or cut stem of a palm or peperomia. The dominant tree — if any single species can be called dominant in such a varied woods — is the towering, broadly buttressed *almendro*, or tonka, the almond-shaped fruits of which litter the ground and surely play a major role in the economy of the forest community. Some creatures are able to crack or chisel the rocklike shells of the tonka beans, but a great number of others simply ignore them until they swell and open with the constant wetting of the rainy season.

Paul has tallied a fair number of mahogany trees, and there is a good sprinkling of *laurel* and *cedro macho*, both valuable wood, and even an occasional *cedro real*, the so-called Spanish cedar, more characteristic of drier forest, and one of the finest timber trees of the American tropics. Here also I saw for the first time in numbers the *pan-subá*, or monkey-pot tree, one of the real giants of the forest, with huge brown fruits like thick-walled pots hanging on long, pendent stems. When a fruit ripens, a circular plug becomes neatly detached at one end to disclose an interior stuffed with seeds somewhat like the seeds of the Brazil-nut tree, to which the monkey-pot is closely related. Monkeys are so fond of the nuts that it is next to impossible to find an open fruit that has not been plundered. This forest has the primeval and somewhat Gothic look of true selva. Game is more plentiful than we have seen it anywhere. The booming call of the curassow can be heard on every side, and each ravine or blowdown tangle has its flock of *pavas*. We found a fine camp site beside a clear rocky creek that gurgles through high woods with almost no marginal tangle.

Shortly after our arrival here, as we were hanging hammocks and building shelters, Sosa suddenly lifted his face to the breeze and began sniffing like a winding coonhound, and with mounting agitation. After a few seconds, he dropped an armful of palm leaves, grabbed his machete, and motioned to me. *¡Wari!* he said. *¡Véngase!* *Wari* is the Mosquito name for the white-lipped peccary, the *chancho de monte*, a big, low-slung wild hog that roves the rain forest in immense bands. As the *wari* move through the woods, they give off a cloud of musky scent that anyone can smell at close hand and that some of the *montañeros* can follow at a dead run. And that is just what Sosa began to do, dashing off among the trees so fast that I was able to catch up only when he stopped for a moment to listen for the herd. Alternately running the scent and stopping to listen, we continued the chase, and suddenly came upon the peccaries. They were eating tonka beans in a shallow ravine. The band as a whole was moving along the ravine bottom, but the individual hogs were milling about and shuttling petulantly back and forth from one tonka tree to another, cracking nuts noisily, and every so often tearing off in a concerted rush for another tonka cluster. Fights broke out sporadically in one part of the host or another, and there was a great deal of clicking and snapping of teeth, which Sosa whispered was directed at us, although the beasts gave no other sign that they were aware of our presence. Keeping behind tree trunks, we had made our way to within a short distance of the nearest of the band when suddenly a half-grown tapir rose from the ground between us and the hogs. *Danto,* whispered Sosa, and we stopped in our tracks. Managing this time to restrain the impulse to shoot point-blank at the looming bulk, I carefully aimed at the base of the poor brute's ear, fired once, and watched the tapir go down. We left it and ran on with the *wari,* which still paid us no heed despite the crack of the twenty-two. After some maneuvering I located a boar in the open and shot him four times before he knew what had happened. He streaked off among the trees with the now alarmed herd, but fell within two hundred yards or so. As we ran up to the fallen animal, I noticed for the first time that my companion carried under one arm a bunch of four-foot sections of the slender stems of the huiscoyol palm. These he had cut as he ran along — evidently almost without pausing, since I had not even been aware of the operation. Each section had been cut by one machete slash at either end, and the slanting bevel across the horn-hard cortex of the cylinder made a murderous javelin. Sosa told me later that in his *hulero* days he had killed several *wari* with these spears when ammunition was scarce, having first located the herds by scent and then induced them to attack him by barking like a dog. How hogs in this wilderness can have come by an overweening prejudice against dogs is not clear, but all hereabouts agree that they have it. When we reached the dead boar, I was astonished at his size and forbidding mien. His weight we estimated at between eighty and one hundred pounds, and the yellow tusks were appallingly long and curved, although worn blunt at the tips. Sosa excised a pair of musk glands from the small of the hog's back and we packed the carcass back to camp, where the entire force joined us to go after the tapir. For supper we had the livers of the *chancho* and the tapir, and the latter, especially, was excellent. Afterward the boys built a frame of green poles over a smoky fire and on it threw a mountain of meat — tapir, *wari,* and some split curassows — covered all with leaves, and said hopefully that this superficial treatment would preserve it for at least a week. Right or wrong, we can do no better, since we have only enough salt for use in cooking.

APRIL 20. We were up before dawn today to pack on ten kilometers farther into the forest to our present camp site, beside a tiny trickle of a brook, which we reached at about ten this morning. Shortly after arriving, Paul, Charlie, and I left for a ten-kilometer timber count through an area that has been held before us by the machete crew as the most promising that their *picadas* have opened up. From what we saw today, however, and even counting in the better score of yesterday, there simply is not enough mahogany in this region to support a commercial operation. The usable trees are so scattered that even with the current price of four hundred dollars a thousand feet, the long haul to the *vega* and the hazardous flood-time float down the racing Huahuashan would eat up the profit. Paul is showing a little professional melancholy over the situation. I remind him that his job is purely exploratory and the dearth of mahogany no fault of his, but I suppose it's depressing to the expert in forest mensuration to deal in inconsequential figures.

Alfaro, who is Company Land Agent and proud of knowing more jungle geodesy than anybody of his acquaintance, left about noon to locate and *"conocer"* the far corner of this tract, which is at the edge of the company holding. He underestimated the distance, and to his utter humiliation was overtaken by darkness far out on the feeble *carril* which ran through open selva and would have been hard to follow even by day. He fired his old pistol several times, and like a good woodsman sat down by a reassuring cut twig to sweat out a hungry night. His shots were almost inaudible in the distance, but by luck one of the boys who had been hunting *gongalola* eggs away from the noise of the camp heard them and ran in much agitated. A rescue party with flashlights went and fetched Alfaro. *El coronel* fancies himself as the toughest of *montañeros,* infallibly versed in the caprice of *madre selva* (which he almost is), but his face brightened visibly when he saw and smelled the huge *wari* stew that Arnold had bubbling over the fire.

It is now sadly clear that the boys were over-optimistic in their hope of preserving yesterday's meat by smoking it in bulk. Some has been sliced and re-smoked, and the rest we are trying to eat up. Some of the men with us have gone six months at a time with almost no break in the monotony of straight *gallo pinto,* and the amount of meat they can consume, to save it, is prodigious.

APRIL 21. We moved camp five kilometers today, making along the way several short cruises at right angles with the main *picada.* As I prowled along by myself, a half mile or so in front of the others, I suddenly found myself in the midst of *wari*. There was a sea of them — maybe a hundred, possibly three hundred — and the rustle and patter of their hard little feet was all about me like the raindrops of a sudden shower. They were foraging for *almendras*, and I had infiltrated their ranks and was surrounded by pigs before I — and I hoped they — knew it. It is well known that these white-lipped peccaries are an unreliable breed, and their numbers make them a formidable force indeed if once they become aroused. They have been called the only really dangerous mammal of the American Tropics. Sosa told me of finding a few bones belonging to an *hulero* friend of his who had set out to infuriate a herd in order to bring them within range of his palm lances. If a tree proper for climbing is at hand, a herd of any size may be provoked with impunity, but in blind underbrush, or among trees too big and smooth to scale, the menace of those yellow tushes is an awful reality. I meditated on all this as the *chanchos* milled about me, either unaware of my timorous presence or for some reason unconcerned by it. I stood still, but my eyeballs rolled about in their sockets in quest of a tree with low branches. Shortly I spied one and moved quietly over to it. Waiting until I had located what looked to be a fat virgin sow, I placed a hollow-point just where the ear swelled back into the neck, and she fell with a slight groan. Another pig scuttled from behind a tree not twenty feet from me and stopped dead still, broadside on. I found the same spot on him and he dropped where he stood. With one hand on the tree I watched the reaction of the herd. A scattered dozen swine had wheeled toward me and stood bristling, gnashing and popping their teeth, and rumbling in their guts; but the rest flowed off among the trees like muddy water from a burst levee, and to my relief the *bravos* quickly calmed down and joined them.

Today we are encamped in a small, sunny clearing made (by felling a single big tree) for the purpose of drying out some of our gear that is suffering from the constant dampness of the twilit forest. Sosa found a young *barba amarilla* (fer-de-lance) under my hammock, which was an event, since reptiles of all sorts have been unbelievably scarce. To date I have collected only four poisonous snakes, and these all of different species: a palm viper, a hog-nosed viper, a pretty coral snake, and the little fer-de-lance just taken.

Ticks have become a nuisance of late, but by repeated dusting of our legs and clothes with a bag of DDT and derris powder, we keep them from doing much damage, although we are usually covered with them. Without an insecticide I don't see how life in some parts of these woods would be possible. In the blowdowns and flood-plain *breña*, where light gets in and grasses grow, there may be a cluster of seed ticks — ravenous hatchlings from a single brood — waiting impatiently on twig tip or grass blade every few feet along the trail. It is impossible to avoid them if one is to make any progress at all. Like all natives of tick country, the local people stop at regular intervals and lash their trouser legs with a cluster of switches or with a dried cow tail that they carry for the purpose; and while this is surprisingly effective, the repeated halts make for slow going, and each time a few ticks get through anyway. Thus, life goes on only because a person slowly builds up an immunity that makes of a tick bite a mere mechanical mishap instead of the inflamed disaster that it may be to the tenderfoot. Most people leave this kind of country before the full flowering of their immunity, but some people can't leave, and these develop a passivity toward ticks that is marvelous to see.

APRIL 22. We have moved back to the camp where I shot the tapir and have named the place "El Danto" in memory of the event. On the trail this morning I came abruptly upon another tapir, evidently full-grown and much bigger than the one I shot. We met on a heavily wooded ridge, and the mountain cow heard or smelled me just as I saw it, and pivoted ponderously to face me with no show of fear, or of any other emotion. It stood no more than thirty feet away and looked straight at me for a long time. I was delighted at the encounter because it gave me a chance to confirm my notion that a tapir is precisely what one would expect of a cross between an elephant and a donkey. I suppose I made a poor impression, however, because the tapir began slowly to lift one forefoot and then the other and pound the earth with resounding strokes, uttering at the same time a whistling neigh a little like that of a startled buck deer but much louder. There was no way of knowing whether these sounds were intended to scare me off, to warn an unseen infant, or to call in reinforcements, but it was clear that the creature was growing dissatisfied with the tête-à-tête. When I moved a bit nearer it gave ground, which secretly pleased me, and when I pressed the advantage the mountain cow backed faster, and then wheeled and trotted slowly away, stopping several times, however, to turn and face me and make the wonderful drumming noise — pom-pom-pom-pom — with it sledge-like front feet. From the tapir-lore that I have picked up around the campfire (Lord knows there's little enough in books) I lean to the theory that this was a female with a calf nearby, and it was mostly this feeling that kept me from shooting it, which I could easily have done. I also cite the abstention as atonement for my irresponsible attack on the first tapir of the ravine mudhole, and claim double credit because I could already feel the sting of the tongue-lashing in store for me when Arnold and the Lagoon boys should hear of my improvidence. No more than fifteen minutes after the pounding of the tapir's feet had died away, I came upon a band of eight *sajinos*, or collared peccaries, scattered on either side of the trail. These wild pigs are somewhat smaller than *wari*, with shorter bodies, longer legs, less yellow tint in the coarse grizzled coat, and with much sharper and more pointed canine teeth, the upper and lower of which slide slantwise into a shearing union that would snip baling wire. They roam in small bands of usually fewer than a dozen, and while they are a scourge of hunting dogs, I have never heard them called a hazard to man; and they are very good to eat. Accordingly, I raised my rifle and shot two of them in rapid succession. The shot pigs squealed, and on the instant the other six started charging back and forth at high speed, emitting a continuous chorus of staccato grunts, and I began to wonder if I should have approached this party with some of the respect demanded by *wari*. Several times a pig passed within a yard or two of where I stood, but all failed to see me and I in turn could not get my sights on them, so fast and erratic was their pace. I was unable to make out whether their volatile behavior was motivated by fear or by rage — whether they were quartering the site in myopic search of an enemy, or had merely become disorganized by fright. I was rooting for the latter, but couldn't rid myself of the feeling that they were looking for me. Finally, however, one after another bounced off in an aimless tangent into the woods, and I was watching the last leave when Paul and Charlie came up. Charlie proceeded forthwith to show the black magic of his woodcraft by quickly finding each of the pigs, trailing them somehow in the deep leafmold that had been scuffed and ploughed for fifty yards by the shuttling herd. One was dead, and the other required a coup-de-grâce. Both lay within two hundred yards of the trail, but if Charlie had not been there I should never have found either.

APRIL 23. When by a quick reconnaissance we found the hinterland becoming progressively less promising, Paul today decided to cut short our stay in the area and return to the river. Accordingly, we moved back to Corozo, taking a route different from that used on the trip out and counting timber on the way. The hike was uneventful, and I passed the time taking inventory of the birds that by virtue of abundance, obtrusive voice, large size, or gastronomic qualities impress themselves upon the notice of the sojourner in the *montaña*. These are as follows: parrots of at least six kinds, including both green and red-blue-and-yellow macaws in abundance; toucans of three sorts, all noisy, gaudy, and ubiquitous; the deceptive and elfin pop-match mentioned earlier; tinamous of two kinds, both crepuscular callers with unearthly voices, and both now nesting and laying improbably huge, blue eggs which we all hunt and eat avidly; curassows and *pavas*, both staples in our diet, the former announcing its presence beside the trail with a vibrant *"voom,"* and the latter possessed of a demoniac voice more like that of a rutting burro than any bird; motmots and trogons, each of several species; pigeons of half a dozen kinds, some walking the forest floor or hurtling in close-winged flight among the tree trunks like ricocheting bullets, others never descending from the high canopy overhead — some that have voices as poignantly sweet as a mourning dove's, and some that bellow like a lost tenderfoot; a skinny wood rail; a small covey-quail and the big painted forest quail that yodels by dark and whose succulence I sang last week; vociferous oropendulas which tumble forward to swing head-down from their perches at each outburst of explosive song; two friendly brown wood hewers with curved bills and much curiosity; and the strange, iridescent big-hummingbird-or-little-kingfisher of which I made a skin several days ago, and which has now become abundant. There are surely some conspicuous birds that I have inadvertently omitted, and there are others that still are only voices to me — and I dare say some of these would be only voices to a trained birdman.

Towering above our camp there is a great tree in which twenty or thirty green macaws are puttering about, squabbling sporadically, and making an obnoxious racket. It is a flock of macaws in pairs; and although the flock itself shows some organization, it is subdivided into duos of presumably mated birds, which fly close together when the group is in flight and feed together when it forages. A tiny creek flows under the treeful of macaws. It is usually clear as air, but two or three times a day — on the word of the boys who stayed in camp while we were back in the bush — muddy water comes down. The mud is said to be stirred up by a tapir that bathes in a pool upstream. Henningham cut a trail from camp back to the pool, thinking that it should be easy to take the cue from the muddy water and sneak back and surprise *tilba* in his tub, but to date he has been too quick. The woods adjacent to the river bottom here show an accentuation of the incongruously youthful look that I have previously referred to, there being a strip at least a mile wide in which the dense stand of skinny saplings suggests nothing more than a ten-year-old *guamil*, grown up after abandonment of cultivated fields. Surely no flood of the Huahuashan could have invaded ground this high to check the normal succession, and the hurricanes that almost certainly have strongly modified the Pearl Lagoon landscapes in general could hardly have skinned off these localized patches. They look insistently like old fields, but the Lagoon people scoff at such a notion and say nobody ever lived on the upper Huahuashan. This is probably not strictly true, since along the river there are scattered clumps of South American *pejibaye* palms which are most likely descended from stock brought in by the same forgotten Indians who carried the edible nuts about and made repeated introductions along the Central American Coast. These people, possibly Sumos, must have inhabited the Huahuashan in pre-Columbian times, and they probably left only when their perennial enemies, the Mosquitoes, burgeoned in Pearl Lagoon under British patronage in the early nineteenth century. Captain Hebbard told me this morning that his grandfather helped "coptyoor-a-wile-mon" on the Huahuashan during the 1870's when he went with a party from Perla to spot canoe trees. On rounding a bend the expedition surprised a man and woman spearing fish from a boulder bar. Both instantly dived and the woman escaped under water; but the man emerged some distance downstream, where the Mosquitoes cornered him against a high bank and took him prisoner. This allegedly occurred five days' journey from the mouth of the river. The man was taken back to Perla as a great curiosity, since no Mosquito of that time had ever seen or heard of a human being from the *montaña* of Huahuashan. The Huahuashan "second growth" must then remain an enigma until some plant ecologist has the opportunity to explore it thoroughly and meditate at length on its manner of origin.

APRIL 24. After much cogitation and some short exploratory jaunts by *cayuca* and on foot, Paul decided today that the timber cruise is officially over. He will cut a few log sections to send up to New Haven, where he expects to do graduate work in the technology of tropical hardwoods next year, but from now on until time for the launch to pick us up downriver we shall loaf and take it easy. When Paul announced this decision the Lagoon boys yelled with delight, since the combination of abundant victuals, steady pay, and good fishing is their idea of Elysium. Even Alfaro, who keeps talking about getting old, poured himself another quart can of coffee and sank into his hammock sighing, *Es rico en la montaña*. Sosa at once set about making himself a rubber dufflebag and invited me to go with him to get the rubber.

To an *hulero*, making a rubber sack is something of a ritual; and after having lived out of a pair of them for three weeks, I was in a suitably reverent mood to serve as acolyte. First we went in search of *hule* trees, and had little difficulty in locating four that appealed to Sosa. With his machete he made a shallow cut across the butt of each tree and inserted in each cut a section of palm leaf to serve as a spout. Climbing the tree he cut a vertical channel from the spout upward for a distance of perhaps ten feet and then slashed a herringbone pattern of slanting tributaries. Almost immediately the whole system of cuts began to ooze shining white latex, and a steady small stream poured from the spout. We went off hunting curassows, and when we returned, the four trees had bled a gallon and a half of sap — more than enough for a sack. When we reached camp, Sosa took five liters of the latex and added a pinch of salt; a teaspoonful of sulphur mixed apart with a little sap and strained into the main container through a rag; three drops of kerosene; and a tiny piece of lard. The sulphur is of course the vulcanizing agent; the other ingredients are supposed to render the rubber immune to deterioration from the effect of common substances with which it might come in contact. (How much of this is religion and how much good chemistry I don't pretend to know.) Sosa complained mildly over having forgotten to bring either alum or castor oil,

a bit of either of which he says gives the rubber a gleaming surface. He next made a frame of suitable size and
on it stretched five yards of unbleached domestic (which
he had packed for twenty days in anticipation of such a
period of leisure). The first coat of rubber he poured on
and spread with his hands over the stretched cloth; at
few-minute intervals he applied second and third coats
and smoothed them by tilting the frame back and forth.
The frame was then placed in direct sunlight; when the
surface of the latex had lost its tackiness, the whole thing
was carefully dipped into the river several times and put
under shelter to remain overnight. Tomorrow Sosa will
give it another exposure to sunlight and then remove the
cloth from the frame, trim it, fold one edge and stick it
back with latex, and use the same mixture to bind the
seams that will give the five yards of material the form
of a broad sack. These sacks are the indispensable carryall
of those who spend much time in the rain forest, and the
vital part they play in spanning the gap between misery
and comfort can hardly be appreciated by one who has
not for days on end had to look into his sack for the only
dry objects in his environment.

We have been blessed in our victualing lately, having
had smoked curassow and *wari* for nearly every recent
meal. Instead of getting tired of them, I merely feel a
little sad that we shall soon leave the woods and return
to prosaic provender. The *wari* is so good that I have
appropriated a hind leg and surreptitiously salted it, and
have been hauling it from camp to camp, each evening
giving it a treatment in a little smokehouse of green palm
leaves. I hope to take it out with me, both as a memento

of my spree in the *montaña* and to prove to my wife that *wari* ham is as good as I shall say it is. The Perla folk are all anxious to get a tapir to smoke and take back for a homecoming celebration, so after supper we paddled upstream to search for eye-shine with my headlight. We failed to locate a tapir, but shined the eyes of several pairs of *micos de noche* (kinkajous) — lighthearted and winning little beasts that screech and whistle in the tall trees along the *vega*. Their eyes reflect fire of almost blinding intensity, and to see them for the first time is to wonder if a panther has taken to the treetops.

Huahuashan

APRIL 25. Today I went fishing — plain old worm
fishing — with Captain Hebbard, Edward Patterson — the
"Judge" of Perla — and Robert Henningham. We paddled
upstream for an hour, beached the boat, and walked out
to an oxbow lake on an old terrace that seems to represent
the flood plain of some earlier erosion cycle. As we sat on
logs and watched our corks, it occurred to me that there
was little in the appearance of my companions to dis-
tinguish them from a party fishing for catfish on the Ogee-
chee River. Even the easy cadence and soft, full vowels
of the Mosquito dialogue of the Captain and the Judge,
gossiping, I guess, about the affairs of their incredible
little town, had a familiar sound — an oddly soft intona-
tion that seems to characterize the speech of older Negroes
everywhere, whatever their language may be. I grew up
in Savannah, where two of the more distinctive Negro
dialects of the southeast, 'Geechee and Gullah, meet. The

first of these is English patois and the latter is an Anglo-African hodgepodge, and although so dissimilar that Gullahs and 'Geechees often cannot understand each other at all (on my honor I several times interpreted for them on the Savannah docks), from a distance they sound much the same. The speech of the Black Caribs of Honduras and the linguistically very different talk of the old and middle-aged Mosquito people are the same quiet music and their English similarly modulated. Moreover, the ancients recognize and decry the difference between their English and that of the young people, seeing in it (as they see in all the misfortune that has befallen their land for three generations past) another baneful effect of Nicaraguan occupation.

The fish bit slowly, and I had plenty of time to listen and to look at Edward Patterson, whose light and somewhat aquiline face was the most interesting of the group. I broke into his conversation with the Captain, and by some maneuvering managed to get him to talk about himself in English. He is, he said, the descendant of an expatriate Scotchman of the same name, who from unknown motives moved to Pearl Lagoon in the 1840's and almost immediately found favor with the reigning King of the Mosquitia, George Augustus Frederick, ultimately being appointed Royal Secretary. By some whimsey the Lagoon people of that time had, in addition to the King, a "President," who it appears was a kind of spare king, responsible for handling affairs of state when the monarch was drunk. The Judge's great-grandfather, Henry Patterson, son of Edward, held this unique office. I showed such interest in all this that Edward was stimulated to remark that he had at home three relics of those golden days: two "king-papers," that is, royal proclamations, signed by George Frederick, and a table the top of which was a single plank hand-hewn from a *gamba,* or buttress-root, of mahogany. The latter was originally four feet wide, but when Nicaragua took over Perla from the English the first *comandante* borrowed the table and trimmed off several inches when it failed to pass through the door of the *comandancia.* Edward related this without passion — as if it were merely what one even yet expects of Nicaraguan officials. He thinks I should buy the table and take it home, and, weird as the idea sounds, perhaps I shall. I could send it to Honduras on the bamboo barge, which makes frequent trips to Bluefields to get *bratarra* prop poles for the North Coast banana plantations.

On our return to camp, Arnold met us with his biggest pot full of *crema de almendra,* just made and cooling in the river. This popular Nicaraguan *refresco* is made of pounded tonka beans, extracted from their shells by soaking and heating. The paste is stirred into enough water to make a thin gruel, and sugar and nutmeg are added. It tastes a little like a vanilla milk shake, and in the *montaña* is nectar indeed. The only thing is, as Arnold suggested, that this may not be a wholly propitious time to drink too deep of the delicious stuff, since tonka beans are rated as a potent aphrodisiac. "Yes, mon," said Arnold, "when they in season we in season!" We recklessly drank all there was, however, and felt no unusual effects.

APRIL 26. Last night two of the Mosquito boys roused me out of my hammock with the proposal that we go fishing again — this time taking my grains, a heavy, two-pronged gig with offset barbs, made in Key West and much coveted by the local fishermen. Interest in this version of a familiar instrument is so strong that I'm having a hard time deciding whom to leave it with when I go away. We stayed out late spearing *tubas*. At night these handsome fish seek shallow, gravelly riffles and congregate in them in great numbers. If startled by noise from an approaching boat they flee en masse, flipping off toward a deep pool or undercut bank in a series of aerial sallies and dives. Many of them bounced off the high sides of the *cayuca*, and one jumped in. By drifting silently down to a *tuba*-riffle we usually managed to impale at least one fish before passing on, and in this way we eventually got fourteen of them. We saw six caimans (which the Mosquitoes call *tura*) and one crocodile (known locally as *carás*). This afternoon, the collective fish-hunger being still unabated, I seined a lot of small shiny characins and went still-fishing with live bait. I caught twelve *guapotes* and had a spectacular battle, much cheered from the bank, with an immense sabalo. It was a one-sided struggle, since I was using a piece of kingfish line and a heavy hook, but the sabalo showed the most bewildering ingenuity while trying to get away and jumped at least a dozen times before finally giving up. After dark, Captain Hebbard paddled me around for an hour or so, and I shot two caimans for the collection. I expect to skin them and clean the skulls during tomorrow's trip downriver.

APRIL 27. This morning, with our junket nearly over, and during what had promised to be a lazy and uneventful run down the river, I had the only real misadventure of the whole trip. I came, I believe, fairly close to meeting with an unattractive end. As I implied some days back, except for a few poisonous snakes, the only creature in these woods that by any stretch of the imagination could be called dangerous is the *wari* — the white-lipped peccary. I had heard this for years and Sosa had known it practically from birth, but the crew was a little melancholy because the last few days had yielded no great store of red meat with which to reinforce our welcome in fish-fed Perla. Thus, when we suddenly found ourselves drifting through a heavy, invisible cloud of *wari* musk, there was a chorus of yells and the whole flotilla turned abruptly and headed for the bank.

As the *cayucas* slid into shallow water we all swarmed ashore. Having seen Sosa's nose in action on a previous pig hunt, I kept as close to him as possible in the rush, and soon the two of us had become separated from the rest of the pack that was quartering the *vega*. Sosa again was following by scent. I could easily detect the odor that led him, but to me it was amorphous vapor while to Sosa it was like a tangible cord being hauled through the woods behind the alarmed and now running *wari*. Pushing along at a steady trot, we covered perhaps half a mile before we began to catch up with the pigs. The first sign that they were near was a little straggling *lechón*, a tiny striped suckling that we almost stepped on; and then we heard the scuttling of countless feet, the popping of pig teeth, and the squeals of other young ones trampled or abandoned in the stampede. Sosa began to collect a sheaf of javelins, hardly slackening his pace as he lopped off and trimmed the palm stems. I noticed that the look of the woods was changing, the ground falling away, and a huiscoyol understory closing in, but for a time I was too intent on the pig hunt to worry about it. Finally, however, I was on the verge of asking Sosa, who was charging ahead with complete abandon, if he didn't think we might overrun the herd and get into trouble, when he stumbled over another infant *wari* and fell heavily upon it. Like any scared pig the *chanchito* made the woods ring with its screams, and suddenly the hoof-rustle ahead of us ceased. I skidded to a stop and looked at Sosa. Up to now his mongoloid face had been lit by an almost fanatical lust for pig meat, but as he harkened to the half-ring of ominous silence out where the hogs should be running for their lives and realized that we had plunged deep into a treeless huiscoyol swamp, he looked decidedly uneasy. Every slender palm stem about us was armed with clusters of four-inch, glass-hard spines, and there was nothing that even a squirrel could climb. We had grossly overreached. Moreover, the sows were farrowing, and we had separated the horde from dozens of sucklings that were now behind us, pattering back and forth in vociferous search of maternal comfort. In this thicket the *wari* had determined to run no farther, and they now stood in an invisible rank before us. Two more tiny waifs bounced up and began to nose Sosa's feet, and I looked down and saw another rooting and butting at my own cheerless boots. Here was boarbait indeed, and, acting on the same impulse to rid ourselves of it, Sosa and I each lifted a *lechón* off the earth in a looping place kick. This, of course, was the last thing we should have done. The sucklings lit shrieking, at no great distance, and the hitherto silent band that opposed us behind the palm-cane screen began to move again — not in retreat this time, but back and forth in restless arcs that ebbed and flowed through the jungle before us, beside us, and soon even behind us. They snapped and gnashed their teeth as they trotted, and I was painfully reminded of the standard situation of western movie melodrama in which mounted Indians circle a doomed and helpless wagon train. A piglet squeaked behind us and a sow careened past me not three feet away. Reflexively, I swung to shoot, but my barrel touched a vine and the bullet struck the hog in a ham. She barged on, grunting and squealing with pain; and suddenly there was a new sound from the band. It was the deep, rumbling blood-voice, half roar, half snarl, of a hundred boars ready to fight. The awesome theme was picked up at first one point and then another until we were nearly surrounded by a wall of sustained and utterly menacing sound. *Ahora, sí, están bravos,* said Sosa. They were mad now for sure. That was what he always wanted, but he seemed to take no joy from it. We could still see nothing of the *wari*, although they were in places perhaps no more than ten feet from us, but it was clear that some, at least, were now standing still, facing us and cursing, and it was a sure thing that they would soon start coming in. I was about to ask Sosa if he thought he could keep the beasts off with his palm spears and machete during the times I should be reloading my ten-shot magazine, when I spied three more sucklings stumping toward us.

I shall always honor the memory of those tiny pigs, because they saved us, at some cost to themselves, from a grisly encounter the outcome of which would have depended largely on whether the people back on the *vega* could have heard our shouts. As the *lechones* trotted up, my plan took shape, and I moved my feet enticingly, at the same time quickly outlining the idea to Sosa. He acquiesced, and together we dived for the sucklings. Sosa got two and I got one, and together we stifled their squeals in my snake bag. Rising to my feet I took one of the pigs from the sack, gagged it with my left hand, and swinging it in a two-handed circle, sailed it as high as I could over the palm tops, far beyond the front rank of the *wari* and in a direction opposite to that from which we had come. It hit the ground screaming, and at once there was a break in the sector of the battle chorus immediately before us, as the hogs wheeled to face this new disturbance. *Otro,* I whispered to Sosa. *Tirálo vos.* Sosa has a better passing arm than mine, and his pig went farther before it landed. Its wild cries drew more *wari* from the wavering ring about us. The mob was disintegrating and there was now no noise at all behind us, toward high ground, while the patter of feet to the sides indicated that many if not all the hogs were converging on the site where the sucklings had landed. *El último,* said Sosa, and I helped him take it from the bag and place it for the throw. As the hapless piglet left his hands, we watched reverently till it climbed to the peak of its trajectory, and then together we breathed *Ya,* and ran like rabbits. There was nothing to oppose us but palm stems, and we kept running till we got out of the huiscoyol and onto high ground with real trees and blessed open vistas where a man could see farther than he could spit. There we stopped to pull out palm spines and get our wind back. *Estaban bravos,* said Sosa when he could talk easily. *Sí, hombre,* I agreed; and we walked away toward the river, thirsty, half-blind with sweat, and full of thoughts and humility.

Pearl Lagoon

*A*PRIL 28. We are back at Perla. We reached Martinez' place last night and found that the launch scheduled to meet us and tow us back to Pearl Lagoon had not arrived. Señora Martinez invited the *jefes* among us — Paul, Alfaro, Henningham, and me — to supper. She served us an egg *torta*, fried beans, the inevitable *cuajada* or cottage cheese, stacks of superb *tortillas*, and papayas; and afterwards we all ate several yards of sugar cane apiece and felt that we had really returned to civilization. Later on I persuaded some of the Lagoon boys to paddle me upstream to try to get a crocodile, as I had not been able to add a skull to the collection. We saw several caimans but only one crocodile — a huge old log of a beast that led us on a long chase but never allowed me a shot. There is a striking difference in the behavior in the water of the crocodile and the caiman. The latter floats or crouches in the shallows with its head held high above the surface, and though it is a relatively small animal, its fully exposed eyes shine with disproportionate brilliance. The crocodile, on the other hand, holds its head so low that the water-line cuts down the reflection from its eyes, and a big one looks little. The caimans stand well for a light and for the approach of a boat, but they are mean and vicious when caught; the crocs are shy and skittish and regular devils inboard. Both are notably more rambunctious than the alligator.

The launch still had not shown up when we finished breakfast, and we set out at 5:30 A.M. to paddle to the Lagoon. It was a long haul, however, and we were glad when at 9 o'clock we rounded a bend and saw a power boat coming up the river. It was the motor *cayuca Esperanza,* a big and fairly shapely dugout with an overlarge engine mounted so high in her that even in smooth water she rolled continuously through many minutes of arc. We were wholly uncritical of her construction, however, when she pushed off downstream at a good clip with our six *cayucas* strung out behind. We had been in the bush exactly one month, and the idea of being towed home was pleasant. Shortly after noon we reached the town of Orinooco, a Carib settlement near the mouth of the river. The existence of a Carib town in the heart of Mosquito territory intrigued Paul and me, and we insisted on stopping to visit it briefly. As we landed, the mob of excited black folk that met us on the low bluff kept shouting for someone named "Sambola," and the Mosquito people with us suggested that we observe protocol and await the arrival of Sambola before beginning our interview. We noticed that while the people spoke English of a sort to us, they addressed each other in the Carib idiom, which though unintelligible was not wholly unfamiliar, since we had often heard it on the North Coast of Honduras. "Can you understand them?" I asked the Mosquito boys. They all shook their heads, and Joe said, "No, thot Ca-reeb, Cop'n." After a while, from one of the palm-thatch houses up in the village a cluster of women emerged, solicitously steering toward us the oldest Negro I ever saw. "Sambola!" everybody yelled happily, and we walked up to pay our respects. To our surprise we found that the old man spoke excellent English. As in the case of the older Mosquito creoles, his speech was softly and elegantly intoned, with more of England than of Jamaica in its accent, and utterly different from the sing-song syllable chains that serve the youthful Caribs and Mosquitoes alike as English. He told us the story of the town. He founded it himself, he said, in 1898, by the simple act of settling on the site with a Sumo woman and begetting so many offspring that in twenty-five years the first generation alone made a respectable village. Nearly all the children stayed in the spreading coconut grove, taking mates from among the creoles, Mosquitoes, or Sumos of the neighborhood; and while the strain got pretty well mixed up, the African genes kept everything else swamped and the language remained that of the Black Caribs. Back in British Honduras, where Sambola was raised in a Carib settlement south of Belize, he had learned some bush medicine from the local *sukia;* and as time went by he extended this lore and became known throughout the Lagoon and as far away as Bluefields and Puerto Cabezas as a medical man. Although he has treatments for nearly anything, he specializes in mental cases, and we were asked to inspect a couple of his current patients. One was a young female idiot from Orinooco; the other a wild looking Indian from across the Lagoon. Sambola obviously had a good deal of professional regard for the pair, but all I could think to say about them was that they certainly must offer quite a challenge. I should like very much to stop at Orinooco for a while and see some of Sambola's methods. There must not be many points of contact with the old Zambo *sukias* left, and their complicated therapeutic systems have had as good a chance for survival here as anywhere along the coast. Who knows what ethnological (and possibly even pharmacological or medical) plums might be picked here if one could only hang around old Sambola for a spell? We photographed the patriarch among a host of his great-grandchildren, which seemed to please him very much. As we left I remembered to ask why he had named his town "Orinooco," and got the unsettlingly logical answer that he had heard that in South America there was a river by that name and had just liked the sound of it!

As the *Esperanza* snaked us out of the river and into the Lagoon, we passed a fisherman poling a *pitpan* along the mangrove shore. He was an arresting figure, evidently almost as old as Sambola, but tall, slim, and straight, with a snow-white beard and skin of salt-frosted jet. He wore only a pair of incredibly tattered trousers and a peaked cap made of the bud-sheath of a palm with the edge rolled back. His tiny dugout seemed as old as he and much more ill-used by time. It was only seven or eight feet long and not much more than a foot wide. One side had long before split off, leaving only two or three inches of free-board at one place; and from stem to stern the little canoe was so worn and eroded that I had to look close to be sure the thing was a boat and not just half a rotting log. The old man stood easily erect in the middle of this comfortless craft and poled it swiftly along with the butt of a fifteen-foot fish spear, the other end of which bore a single-tined, many-barbed head. The Lagoon boys called to the ancient man and he bowed from the waist to us. Paul asked whether he was a Mosquito or a Carib, and Joe said that he didn't know — that he was just a poor man. He was more than that; he was an image that I shall not soon forget.

The run across the Lagoon took us three hours. There was a stiff breeze and a chop offshore that kept us wet most of the time, but it was a beautiful afternoon — one of those rare days that come only in the tropics and after rain, with the sky and sea one shade of burning, *gongalola*-egg blue, and the big, shining clouds sailing in on the trade wind from the sea beyond the *coco*-fringed reef, over the cotton-strewn Lagoon and up the tilted land, to roll over the crests of the distant cordillera. Everybody was in high spirits except Alfaro and Arnold, who, it appears, had been quietly nursing a feud for a long time, and who now that we are out of the woods feel less constrained to hide their spleen. When we were within half a mile of the beach at Perla the *cayuca* crews could restrain their enthusiasm no longer, and one after another they cut loose from the tow-train and struck out for the shore under paddle power. At first the race set Mosquito against "Spoñamon," and as the black and brown backs bowed over the lance-shaped, mahogany paddles the shafts bent and the *cayucas* foamed through the water as though they had just come alive. Two canoes manned wholly by Lagoon boys at once took the lead. As they slid out in front, making the race a home-town competition, the two crews put on an exhibition of paddling the like of which I never expect to see again. There was a shouted signal, and on the instant each of the paddlers rose to a crouching position, raised his paddle behind him, and smacked it hard on the surface of the water with a noise like a pistol shot. Then rising to their feet and reaching forward in perfect unison the thirteen men in the two boats stabbed the water with the thin blades and, as if geared together, jerked a short backstroke that ended in a flipping twist so strong that it rent the surface with a ripping sound and showered sparks of water high above each racing dugout. As the paddle blades disengaged, they were slapped back against the water with a crash before being moved up for the next stroke, which was called by a shrill falsetto and somewhat bloodcurdling cry, surely come down intact from some predaceous ancestor. The pace seemed impossible to maintain, but instead of slackening, it increased, and as the slender dark logs glided closer to the shore and the crowd gathered there began to cheer, the wet black backs stepped up their rhythm to a peak. *Chuk-vop* went the paddles, and *ay-eeee* shrilled the coxswain — *chuk-vop, ay-eeee, chuk-vop, ay-eeee. . . .* The spume and rain from each upstroke were in the air before the drops from the previous stroke had fallen; and as if to complete the glory of the stem-even finish, the hot slanting rays of the sun struck a bright rainbow from the silvery shower above each hissing dugout.

Fifteen minutes later we were ashore, scattered in the deep shade beneath the sprawling mango trees to watch a swarm of volunteer longshoremen unload our gear. The Judge caught a young black relative of his and set him to keeping Paul and me supplied with jelly-coconuts, which we ate with spoons cut from their own rinds. Cashews were in season, and several people brought us palm fiber sacks of the juicy acid fruits, which are a specific for a salt-water thirst. The cashew seeds (the familiar cashew nuts), which protrude from one end of the fruit in such a way as to cause all who see one for the first time to laugh, are usually discarded here, since they are edible only after careful roasting. When we seemed grieved over the lack amid such profusion of raw material, Joe ran up to the house of a woman known to be addicted to them and shortly afterward returned with a bag of nuts that might have come from the corner drugstore. After we had temporarily assuaged our bush hunger, Paul, Alfaro, and I walked over to the Chinaman's where we were shown to our quarters — a cot-strewn room over the cluttered store. Arnold, who will continue to cook for us, set up his kitchen in an adjoining shed and baked a layer cake to celebrate our return. The Chinaman sent us a bottle of rum (which he later put on the bill) and some good limes, but no ice. Away back up the river Paul had half promised the gang a homecoming party when we should arrive in Perla, but he has now wisely retracted.

Although on the river there was little discernible friction between the Mosquito and Nicaraguan components of the expedition, their natural distaste for each other has today come to the surface, beginning with the spat between Alfaro and Arnold that I mentioned earlier. Our main concern now is to keep Henningham's and Alfaro's Spanish Indians as much out of the public eye as possible, since with *guaro* flowing among both elements any argument might set off fireworks. Sosa is very levelheaded (except when chasing pigs) and, though somewhat pickled, he saw the point when Paul asked him to help keep the "Spoñamons" from provoking the Perla people, who after dark had congregated in front of the store to drink *guaro* and sing Moravian hymns and raise a terrific uproar. All this was too much for Charlie, however, and he grew more belligerent by the hour, stalking around the back yard muttering *a la puta* and *jodidos*, fingering his machete, and working up a case of ulcers over the state of things. Shortly after supper we thought we were in the middle of it. Paul was dickering over finances with the Chinaman and I was out back looking for the privy. Suddenly there was a crash, a volley of Spanish and Creole oaths, and an awful shriek from the kitchen, and Alfaro burst from the door screaming to heaven, *¡Soy de raza! ¡Soy de sangre! ¡Si tengo pistola lo mato!* (*sic!* meaning: I am an aristocrat! I am a thoroughbred! If I had a pistol I'd kill him!), with Arnold behind him doubled over in pain, but making every effort to throw a heavy kitchen knife at the retreating colonel. Paul hurtled from the back door, every inch the leader of the expedition, and tackled Arnold, shouting orders so thunderous and profane that Alfaro stopped in his flight, the Chinaman cringed in the shadows of his unlighted store, and even the merrymaking out front was hushed. Alfaro spotted me and rushed over in tears to tell his story in a storm of Castilian rhetoric and I steered him into the store, where out of sight of Arnold he might finally calm down. He had hit Arnold with an iron skillet, (apparently breaking at least one rib) because Arnold had insulted him, and he would never again eat Arnold's cooking. When all the facts were out, it was clear that neither party could be definitely named as the aggressor. The altercation was just a minor flare-up of the old malady, the perennial "Mosquito Question," that for three centuries and more has fermented along this eccentric shore. There was no one to blame or to fire. There was just the peace to keep.

APRIL 29.   This morning Paul had to work on his payroll, so I borrowed the *Esperanza* and her two-man crew, and with Joe went on a sightseeing tour of two other villages on the Lagoon shore. Neither of these is nearly as large as Perla, and both are more strongly Indian and less creole in character. At Raidapura, for instance, Mosquito appears to be spoken almost exclusively, although many of the people are fluent in English and more or less so in Spanish as well. Although Negroid features are still predominant, brown skins and straight hair are more frequently seen than in Perla. The town is composed mostly of crudely built stick-and-manaca huts, but there are two or three beautifully made wattle houses in which the ingenious woven-stick construction of the walls and the deep, highly pitched roof of neatly bound palm make as attractive primitive architecture as I have seen anywhere. On an ash heap I noticed the shell of a species of mud turtle that seemed to me not to belong to this region at all. It was much like the high-shelled stink jims of the interior mountains and clearly unrelated to the flat species common in the coastal plain. When I picked up the carapace for a closer look, a woman who was watching from a nearby doorway motioned to me and pointed suggestively into the house. I walked over and peered in, and on a low brazier saw another mud turtle of the same kind stewing back-down in its shell and swollen to bursting with internal steam. The woman thought I was hungry. When I explained that I wanted a live mud turtle instead of a charred, desquamated, and tender-cooked specimen, she seemed to comprehend the words but was a bit put out at my perversity until I commented that I wished to make medicine out of the creature. I hope to get some specimens of this turtle because there is a good chance that it is something fancy, herpetologically speaking. We could find no more at Raidapura, however, and we left for a run down the roughening lagoon to Cacabila, a curious little village of what appear to be nearly pure Indians. The houses here are widely scattered about an open savanna and without the dense forest of coconut palms that shade the other towns. We were met by a crowd of women and children, but saw no men except an old white Catholic missionary and a Raidapura Indian school teacher furnished by the Nicaraguan government. The missionary was a surprise, since throughout most of the Mosquitia the Moravians are almost the only active sect and the only enlightening influence in the lives of hundreds of Indians and Creoles from Pearl Lagoon to Caratasca and the Patuca back country. Stressing good works more than theology, these energetic, practical, and courageous people have during the past hundred years spread throughout the shore to bring glimmerings of hygiene, nutrition-sense and practical agriculture, effective medical care and training in home economics, carpentry, and rural ethics to communities so remote that but for the Moravians they would literally still be gangs of howling savages. Although *coco*-palms were few in Cacabila there were various other fruit trees growing about the village, and everywhere we went children climbed them to get fruit for us. The cashews were the largest I had ever seen and I ate them to the point of foundering. An infant staggered up to dangle before us a long leguminous pod with a black, sticky, laminated interior. Joe seized this with enthusiasm and handed it to me, declaring that the day was complete now that I could try a "stinking-toe," as he reassuringly called it. To be cooperative, I chewed a bit of the sweetish endocarp, but an utterly loathsome stench so dominated the otherwise date-like character of the pulp that I was unable to continue. Joe assured me that the fruit is delicious once you have got the hang of it. The same thing is said about the East Indian durian; but I, who am as open-minded a victualer as one is likely to come across, am unable to enjoy eating durians, or even getting near them, and this "toe" thing is much the same sort of outrage. Joe was disappointed, and the little Indian was grieved; but after a while we stopped under a star-apple tree and my zest for this really first-class fruit placated them somewhat.

Nearly all the people we saw had light complexions and straight hair, and the girls were quite likely-looking —

or perhaps I had been in the woods too long to judge. However, all over twelve years old (and some under) were either pregnant or nursing, and this prompted me to ask where the men were. They were off planting, I was told, this being the time for the annual slash-and-burn attack on the *montaña* that is the almost universal agricultural regimen along the coast. In this seaboard village, as in most of the other Lagoon towns, there is little nearby land suitable for growing the staple *yaura* (yuca═cassava) which, along with coconut oil, squash, bananas, and fish, forms the bulk of the local diet. The good land lies back of the coastal marshes — up the creeks and rivers — five, ten, or even twenty miles by dugout from home; and here the men go just before the short, fickle dry season, to fell the trees in a patch of *vega* timber. When the rains slacken and the foliage of the fallen trees withers, the patch is fired, and the ash-rich spots between the trunks are planted. It is next to impossible to use the same ground for two successive years, as there is no known way of clearing it of the wild vine-*breña* and sapling thickets that invade the clearing immediately in a mad scramble for the new space and light. Thus, year after year the Mosquitoes go farther from home to plant and tend their *wari*-ridden subsistence plots, and gardening expeditions involving sojourns in the bush of several weeks are accepted as routine. By the time we left Cacabila the wind had risen to a near gale and was kicking up whitecaps all over the Lagoon. Even with a load the motor-*cayuca* was unstable, and now with a high sea running and her center of gravity up somewhere between her gunwales, she made most of the trip on her

beam ends. My companions fell easily into the routine of
springing from one side to another to right the insane
craft after each roll, but to me it was like a first trip by
tandem bicycle on a slack wire; and I soon left the bal-
ancing to Joe and the crew and just cowered in the mounting bilge. We reached Perla at last, to my surprise, and
as we drew up beneath an overhanging mango tree the
engineer piped without rancor, "This-bod-do-ree-for-
rough-wa-teah, mon." Edward Patterson, the Judge, was
waiting on shore to take me to his home and show me
the ancestral table with the *gamba* top that he had told
me about up the river. Its virtues were hidden beneath
the scars and tobacco burns of a century, but after taking
a look at the crumbling kitchen which the family wanted
to repair with the proceeds from the sale, I offered twelve
dollars for the table and got it. I admired the Judge's king-
papers and some other heirlooms, and then walked across
town to the home of an old man who carves rosewood,
which is abundant hereabouts. The local rosewood is very
dark, reddish-brown and black, and hard as horn. I tried
to persuade the old man to promise to make a whole set
of salad bowls and send them to me in Honduras by the
missionary, but I could awaken no enthusiasm for the
project. I bought a box sculptured from a single chunk
of rosewood and moseyed back to the Chinaman's to
supper. In accordance with his threat, Alfaro was having
no more truck with Arnold's meals, and though still lodg-
ing with us he had hired a woman in a nearby house to
cook for him.

It was quiet outside after supper, and we went to bed
early, but before I had fallen asleep I heard Joe calling

me from the door at the head of the narrow stairs. I got up and groped my way across the dark loft toward the light of his cigarette. He wanted me to go with him to a "Maypole" in a little settlement a mile or so up the lagoon shore. I head heard a lot about these Maypoles ever since reaching the Mosquitia. The people like them so much they always begin having them early in April, and they were in the near offing back in Bluefields when we went through there a month ago. They are dances, held outdoors at night and usually in a grove or under a big tree. The music is furnished by guitars and drums, with whatever supporting instruments may be available, and there is usually plenty of Nicaraguan rum or of *chicha* — a potent local punch. The dance starts as a spirited and highly sexualized exhibition by some exceptionally gifted couple, and stimulated by the erotic antics of this pair other couples soon join in. As it grows, the dance becomes progressively more energetic and relaxed, the force of the music picks up and the tempo mounts till the driving beat has lost itself, to the white ear, in a maze of African subrhythms. By and by all the boys and girls are either dancing or have moved off a respectable distance into the darkness beyond the firelight. Although these parties are uninhibited affairs, much bemoaned by the missionaries, the people are in no way self-conscious about them. Our versatile cook, Arnold Hodgson — bearing one of the most respected names in Bluefields — is a champion Maypole leader; and when Joe whispered his invitation to me last night it was not from shame at the proposal that he spoke no louder, but out of courtesy to the sleepers in the room. I was tired last evening and, faced with a long hot trip

by open *cayuca* back to Bluefields the next day, I fool-
ishly refused Joe's invitation; but I walked with him as
far as the savanna beyond the edge of town, and we stood
there and listened for a while. Over the low rush of breeze
through distant thousands of *coco*-palms we could hear
the pulse of the Maypole drums and the sporadic shouts
of the merrymakers. I pondered on the strange compost
of race and rite that this spring festival represented. By
what devious routes had battle dances and green-corn
ceremonies of lost Sea-Carib and Paya tribes, the "big-
drunks" of the old Zambos, and the rhythm orgies of the
Congo Basin converged here, in the ridiculous name,
Maypole, with the phallic festivals of Asia and the Beltein
sex fests of ancient Ireland? Here, in the spring cotillions
of these Baldan Mosquitoes, were the old fertility rituals
come full circle: from phallus to phallic symbol to chaste,
ribbon-strung pole with the second grade skipping about
it, and now, on the shore of Pearl Lagoon, back to the
phallus unadorned save by the name, Maypole. Not May
Dance, or Maypole Dance, or Mayday Festival — just
Maypole. The bizarre coincidence probably has some
quite prosaic explanation, although none of the several
people with whom I have discussed the matter have been
able to elucidate it. My own guess is that it is the result
of a gesture by early Moravian missionaries (who first
came here from Jamaica a hundred years ago) to dilute
the impiety of endemic orgies that they were unable to
eradicate, by applying to them the name of an innocuous
and similarly timed festival of the homeland. Since the
Mayday ceremonies of that day had probably lost much
of their original functional significance, it seems likely that

the missionaries never even realized the subtle fitness of the imported term; but no doubt the Druids would be gratified with the way the Mosquito Maypoles keep the birth rate up.

I could have stood indefinitely listening to the Maypole and meditating upon it, but I could see that Joe was in a lather to be off and I said, "Well, so long, Joe. Have a good time." "Sure, Cop'n," said Joe, grinning happily; and he turned and trotted off, following the sound of the drums across the dark savanna, and after a bit I made my way back through the quiet village to the Chinaman's loft and bed.

APRIL 30. At nine this morning we finished a round of farewells and took leave of Perla in the *Esperanza* with five *cayucas* in tow. One of these belonged to the Moravian missionary, Mr. Sheimer, who took this opportunity to get to Bluefields for his periodic visit to headquarters. He usually goes with one paddler in the stern and an umbrella against sun and rain, and was understandably pleased to be able to make in six hours a journey that normally took a day and a half. I felt sentimental pangs as we pulled away from the beach with its old leaning mangoes and tall *coco*-palms and the friendly crowd of black folk watching from under them. Perla is a lazy, happy town, where poverty does not necessarily result in malnutrition, and where a high incidence of gonorrhea is surely balanced by a dearth of psychosomatic ills. We reached Bluefields at 3:30 P.M. after a hot trip in a dead calm, with the sun blazing the whole way. The people who welcomed us on the dock seemed a bit surprised that the party had returned intact, and I noticed several of them covertly counting heads; but the cans of cold beer they handed us — and a second-story guest room with clean sheets and a lagoon breeze — erased, for the time, all regret for folded jungle hammocks and the lost, cool gloom of the tall *montaña*.

*   *   *   *   *   *

PAUL had to stay in Bluefields to complete his report, but the next day I got a reservation on the noon plane to Managua. I spent the morning looking up Henningham, Alfaro, Arnold, and such of the Spanish Indians as were still scattered about town, shaking their hands, and vowing to be back almost immediately. At two o'clock Paul went with me to the air field and saw me aboard the DC-3 just in from the Cape. The pilot was a man by the name of Al whom I had met back in Tegucigalpa. The plane was nearly empty, with only a sick Indian and a hodgepodge of light freight aboard, and Al suggested that I move up into his sacred capsule in the nose and keep him company.

I sat on a stool between Al and his slim Nicaraguan co-pilot and watched the scrub at the end of the little airstrip rush at us on a take-off that seemed to clear the trees by inches. The land quickly slipped back under us and we skimmed out over Bluefields Lagoon. Al put us into a climbing turn and, looking back at the rows of empty seats behind us, said, "Anything you want to see on the way over?"

"Sure," I answered, "the Huahuashan."

"Too far north," said Al. "We'd get in late and I'm on probation already."

217

"How about Río Cama then?" I compromised. "Let's fly up the Escondido to the Cama, follow it a way, double back, and head for Rama and the Siquia-Mico junction, fly low over El Recreo, and then head for home. Would that show on your gas gauge?"

"O.K.," said Al.

This erratic course would take us over the agricultural experiment station at El Recreo and the huge United Fruit oil palm plantation on the Escondido, and we would see a swatch of the best rain forest north of the Orinoco; but I had another idea in mind. I wanted a last look at the Huahuashan from the air, and this way I might wangle it. Four hundred feet above the water, we roared up the Escondido estuaries and entered the main stream, and before I expected it the mangroves had given way to *montaña* and the mouth of the Cama was beneath us. We banked to the northward to follow it, and as we climbed slowly the ground began to spread and the forest roof to smooth out. There were clusters of houses along the *vega*, and I remembered the redoubtable *hulera*, Juana Alvarez, and her house on the Cama, and wondered which it was, and how living in a house suited Juana.

At two thousand feet Al levelled off and we all looked out to admire the view of the coastal plain. At that height the texture, tint, and contour of the individual trees were softened but not lost, and the rolling canopy looked like a field of velvet balls, of every shade of green, floating three-deep on a sea that spread before us to the northern horizon. Isolated masses of tan or reddish-brown were buried among the greens, and here and there, each separated from the next by miles of forest, there was a splash of glowing yellow where a cortez tree was in flower.

As I looked out over the ocean of vegetation, I noticed intermittent flashes of brilliant light, coming apparently from somewhere above the treetops. Although the tiny bursts of fire seemed to come from point sources, and gave no hint as to the area of the reflecting surface, they were bright blue in color. When I asked Al if the monkeys were signalling us from the high twigs, he replied without hesitation, "Butterflies," and I realized at once that he must be right. The flashes must be butterflies — huge morphos flitting about, in and above the top forest level and changing the sun to hot turquoise on the metallic surfaces of their wings. I marvelled that the small area of a butterfly wing could throw back to our height light so intense and so strong in color. Al was unimpressed, however, and assured me that he had seen the same thing from as high as eight thousand feet!

We had left the dim mound of Cukra Hill in the southeast and the Cama was shrivelling into the Pichinga. As we began the slow circle that would put us on the course to Rama, I got up from my seat and went back into the body of the plane and pressed my nose against a north window. Beyond the Cama tributaries I could see a master stream heading for Pearl Lagoon. That would be Río Patche; but this was not far enough. I lifted my gaze still more and with stubborn nostalgia swept the far *montaña*. Down where the Patche was broad there was nothing but forest north of it, but as I traced its course upstream I could see a break in the green beyond it and an arc of silver that curved down from the north and did not join the Patche.

This was where I had been. Out there were the halls of the mountain cow, where the *montaña* was even now stealing back into our clearings and hiding the cold ashes of our camp fires; and I watched till the last glint of silver sank into the sea of green and the circling plane turned its tail toward Huahuashan — River of Racing Water, and river of many a dream to come.

El Zamorano in the semi-dry Yeguare River valley of Honduras looking toward the cloud-forested peak of Cerro Uyuca, department of Francisco Morazán. Elevation 790 meters (2600 feet).

The San Juancito cloud forest, department of Francisco Morazán, seen from elevation of 2135 meters (7000 feet), one of several cloud forested peaks visible from El Zamorano. Photo by Margaret Hogaboom.

Tree ferns inside the Cerro Uyuca cloud forest.

The author and his wife, Marjorie, examining the mosses and epiphytes on the bole of a cloud forest tree on Cerro Uyuca.

Mature hardwood cloud forest on Cerro Uyuca, department of Francisco Morazán. Elevation 1860 meters (6100 feet).

This little *milpa* or cornpatch on the edge of the cloud forest of El Volcán is planted with corn in individual holes among the recumbent tree trunks. It will be abandoned after a few seasons and allowed to revert to thickets of brush, vines, and saplings of *guamil*.

Casita or thatched hut in the *milpa*. However, the farmer who built it told the author that he walked home every night in order to avoid *comelenguas* (see page 38).

The wasting land, department of Francisco Morazán. Diamond checking was made by feet of generations of grazing cattle. Elevation 790 meters (3600 feet).

Pinabetes (Pinus pseudostrobus) covered with epiphytes just below the cloud forest on Cerro Uyuca, department of Francisco Morazán, elevation 1585 meters (5200 feet).

Ocotal (Pinus oocarpa), the most widespread pine forest in Honduras. These pine forests grow on well-drained slopes at elevations of roughly 610 to 1370 meters (2000 to 4500 feet).

The author in the mixed scrub forest at the edge of the Yeguare River Valley.

Choluteca River, one of the largest rivers in Honduras, department of El Paraíso. Elevation about 800 meters (2650 feet).

Flood plain forest along the Yeguare River, department of Francisco Morazán. Elevation 790 meters (2600 feet).

A *quebrada*, or dry gulch, coming down into the Yeguare River valley.

The Yeguare River, tributary of the Choluteca, which flows into the Pacific Ocean.

Students working the school's farm. Young men from all over Latin America came to study agriculture here. Photo by Wilson Popenoe.

Administration building of Escuela Agricola Panamericana, El Zamorano. Photo by Wilson Popenoe.

Buildings of Escuela Agrícola Panamericana in El Zamorano nestled in a coyol palm grove in the semi-arid valley of Río Yeguare, department of Francisco Morazán. Elevation 790 meters (2600 feet). The road to the left leads to Danlí, the one to the right to the mountain town of Güinope, department of El Paraíso.

It was a wonderful place for children, there in the valley. Chuck, Steve, Mimi, and Tom Carr—and boa constrictor.

Our home at Escuela Agricola Panamericana.

Doña Moncha cooking at her stove in the kitchen of her restaurant, *Casa Grande*, one of the pleasant assets of El Zamorano. Photo by Margaret Hogaboom, 1947.

Doñ Moncha removing cookies from the big outside oven at *Casa Grande*. To heat the oven a fire was burned inside until the thick clay walls were hot. Photo by Margaret Hogaboom, 1947.

Street scene in San Antonio de Oriente.

San Antonio de Oriente, an old silver mining town in the mountains of Honduras, department of Francisco Morazán, it could be reached only by foot or horseback.

Men threshing red beans in San Antonio de Oriente.

Farm in the high hills around the Yeguare Valley. Photo by Marjorie Carr.

The source of water for the town of Juticalpa, department of Olancho. Elevation 610 meters (2000 feet). See page 82.

A natural pasture on the savanna land in Lepaguare Valley, department of Olancho. Elevation 610 meters (2000 feet).

Olancho ponies with brass stirrups and tail-dallied lassos.

Northern end of Lake Yojoa, department of Comayagua, looking toward Cerro Santa Barabara, department of Santa Barbara. Elevation at water level 610 meters (200 feet), at highest peak 2590 meters (8500 feet).

Right: Rain forest on the
Atlantic coast, Valley of Río
Blanco, department of Cortéz.
The small clump of palm at left
is *huiscoyol* (*Bactris major*).
Elevation 180 meters (600 feet).
Bottom: Waterfall in cloud
forest in Central Honduras.

A mountain stream in Central Honduras.

Gulf of Fonseca, looking from Honduras toward El Salvador. Photo by
Margaret Hogaboom.

The crater of Momctombo Volcano, Pacific coast of Nicaragua.

Portage on the Río Huahuashan, on the Atlantic Coast of Nicaragua. Photo by Paul Shank.

Hammocks slung for a one-night camp deep in the Huahuashan primeval forest, or *selva*. Photo by Paul Shank.

The author preparing a speciman in the jungle. Photo by Paul Shank.

Index